# The Economies of Eastern Europe

## IN A TIME OF CHANGE

# The Economies of Eastern Europe

## IN A TIME OF CHANGE

by Adam Zwass

LONDON AND NEW YORK

First published 1984 by M.E. Sharpe

Published 2015 by Routledge
2 Park Square, Milton Park, Abingdon, Oxon OX14 4RN
711 Third Avenue, New York, NY 10017, USA

*Routledge is an imprint of the Taylor & Francis Group, an informa business*



**Library of Congress Cataloging in Publication Data**

Zwass, Adam.
The economies of Eastern Europe in a time of change.

Partial translation of: Die Planwirtschaft im Wandel der Zeit.
Includes bibliographical references and index.
1. Europe, Eastern—Economic policy. 2. Central planning—Europe, Eastern. 3. Europe, Eastern—Economic conditions—1945- . I. Title.
HC244.Z6913 1983 338.947 83-17537

ISBN 13: 9780873322454 (hbk)

# Contents

# Preface

If despite the abundant literature on the subject I venture to present this book to the reader, it is to give a more complex description of the problems than has previously been available, to shed light on the contradictions in the most recent developments, and to discuss the latest attempts to resolve them. I have tried to render events in Eastern Europe comprehensible and to enumerate the advantages of economic cooperation between East and West. I have undertaken this study as an insider with long years of experience as an economist and a writer.

The original German book is in two parts, only the second of which is included in this English version. The first part deals with the problems common to all planned economies, their various stages of development, and their efforts at reform. The second part, presented here, explores the problems specific to each of the socialist countries. Although the past histories of these economies are surveyed in broad terms, the main emphasis is on current economic problems. The achievements of the Sturm und Drang period are described, a period when the economic growth in Eastern Europe astonished the world; but the analysis of the current difficulties and their causes is the focal point of the book.

In a number of instances I have ventured a comparison of the centrally planned economies with the market system. Despite high growth rates, none of the small East European countries has achieved the economic level of Sweden or Austria. The system born and developed in the backward economy of postrevolutionary Russia was entirely inadequate for the German Democratic Republic (GDR) and Czechoslovakia, already industrialized before World War II. These countries have lost rather than gained ground in the family of nations.

The investigation makes clear that the system of central planning and steering, which could be useful in the initial industrialization period, when it was capable of achieving a high rate of "primitive accumulation" at the expense of consumption, is unable to promote the more sophisticated industrialization needed today. The attempt to close the technology gap with the help of the imported know-how and credits from the West has, of necessity, been unsuccessful. The heavy imports without a change in the obsolete steering system have caused an unsupportable debt burden, which impedes further imports. In this connection, the inferiority of the monetary and credit system of the planned economies is examined. Shaped by the autarkic concept of development, it is totally inadequate in a period of developed foreign trade. In relations with the West, the export and import structures of the East European countries are underdeveloped; in credit relations, these countries are only borrowers, not lenders.

The modest reform capabilities and the fate of radical reform attempts resulting from mass movements in Poland, Hungary, and Czechoslovakia are examined in detail. These were doomed to fail not only as a consequence of the external interference but (as in Poland in 1956 and 1980) because of the stubborn resistance of the ruling elite. The bold attempt of Hungary to decentralize economic competences in an unchanged political dictatorship of the Communist Party is discussed.

The analysis of the economic development in the other East European countries culminates in a description of the economic and political crisis in Poland as clear evidence of a crisis of the system, a crisis common to all countries in this group.

The last chapter of the book examines the economic and political aspects of this relatively young system, which, owing to its modest capabilities to adapt the ruling model to external and internal conditions, devastates scarce resources in very expensive production relations and in the manufacture of heavy armaments. This dooms the East European countries to a low living standard. A willingness to reform the obsolete system and to cooperate with the capitalist environment could create enormous possibilities for a further economic and social development of Eastern Europe.

I have tried to make my presentation of the problem as comprehensive as possible so that all who are interested in events in the East may find it useful.

I express my cordial thanks to my friend Gunther Reiman, President of the International Report, New York, for his fruitful encouragement; to Dr. Eveline Elliott, for reading through the text; to Mrs. Anita Deutsch, for providing a neatly typed version of a manuscript that may often have seemed illegible; and to my wife, Friederike, for her extensive help in completing the book.

I dedicate this book to my wife, Friederike, my son Vladimir, and my daughter-in-law, Alicia.

Adam Zwass

# The Economies of Eastern Europe

## IN A TIME OF CHANGE

# 1

# Hungary's Economic Reform Viewed in the Context of Its Political System

The economic and political system imposed by the Soviet Union on all the countries of the Eastern bloc suited none of them, but least of all Hungary. For this country, poor in raw materials, active participation in the international division of labor was a *conditio sine qua non* for its economic existence, which had been placed in jeopardy by the model of autarkic development and the inadequate economic mechanisms of a planned economy. It is therefore not surprising that Hungary was the country that resisted most strongly the economic system imposed upon it.

The people who in the mid-'60s wanted to reform the centrally administered economy were by no means successors of the courageous fighters of the revolt of October 1956. They were pragmatists; they had no desire to tamper with the foundations of the system, and gave judicious consideration to the country's geopolitical situation. The reform they initiated on 1 January 1968 was modestly referred to in official terms as the "new economic mechanism." Although its initiation did indeed coincide with the "Prague Spring," it was not frustrated by the defeat of the latter. This bold experiment, which extended far beyond the confines of a centrally administered economy, was permitted to continue because, in contrast to the Prague Spring, it accommodated itself to the existing political regime. This, however, imposed certain limits upon it.

The history of this experiment, which has now gone on for 15 years, clearly shows how an economic system can be decentralized within a one-party regime. While the reformers were steadily endeavoring to extend the limits of the reform, the opponents of the reform were tirelessly trying to force the steering system back into the traditional channels of a centrally administered economy.

A huge country, rich in natural resources, can exist even with an inauspicious steering system and a model of heavy industry based on inflated accumulation rates, even though this be at the cost of the quality of life of the population. But a model that aimed at transforming a small country such as Hungary into a land of "iron and steel" condemned it to immense losses on the world markets because of faulty economic mechanisms could not maintain itself over the long term. Output required excessive spending on investment projects and labor. More and more forints had to be used to pay for the foreign exchange earned in foreign trade in order to produce export goods. The cost of the 46 percent economic growth and 41 percent growth in consumption in the period between 1958 and 1965 was a 97 percent increase in investment. During the same period, state subsidies to foreign trade increased by 91 percent, and economic growth declined from a 7.9 percent annual average between 1958 and 1960, to 5.6 percent in the years 1960 to 1963, to 4.3 percent between 1963 and 1966.[1]

Hungary's pragmatic party leader, Janos Kadar, understood quite well that under such conditions a reversion to the chaotic conditions of 1956 was a real threat. It was his view that the Hungarian people would perhaps accept a one-party system, but not a *dirigist* national economy, afraid of innovation, cut off from the rest of the world, with stagnating consumption on top of it all, and that decentralized administration of the economy could be made compatible with a totalitarian government. The reform was carefully and meticulously prepared over the course of three years. It was initiated on 1 January 1968 under the modest appellation of "the new economic mechanism." There were many setbacks and many mistakes, but all in all, it may now be regarded as successful. Its principal merit was that it freed firms from the rigid directives and day-in, day-out surveillance of central authorities and gave them a certain margin for independent activity and initiative. It broke new ground, and could have served as a model for the other Eastern countries. It would surely have been even more successful if the decentralization of the steering of the economy had been accompanied by a democratization of political power. This, however, was not the case. For the liberals it was tailored too narrowly; for the conservatives it went too far. Nevertheless, the Hungarian reformers — Nyers, Fock, Csikós-Nágy, Vajda — will go down in history as fighters in the vanguard for a better economic model in Eastern Europe.

The Hungarian economic reform differs from the reforms in the other Eastern bloc nations in the consistency with which it was implemented, but hardly in its fundamental principles. It certainly did not entail a transformation of production relations. What distinguishes the Hungarian reform from the reforms of the other nations is the determination of the reformers to follow the path embarked upon to the very end.

The idea that a central plan was no longer to function as an absolute command inevitably shook the command apparatus at its foundations. Plant and firm managers could take a deep breath. Not all, however: many plant managers, who over the years had become accustomed to the life of a state official, who had everything handed to them and did not have to be concerned about the sale of their products and the expansion of their enterprises (the money for capital investment came from the state coffers and did not have to be paid back) experienced no relief at suddenly being burdened with the responsibility for their enterprise and having to rely on their own initiative.

The central plan was considered a guideline. The plan targets, however, were no longer to be set for individual enterprises. Enterprises were accountable for their operations, but were no longer in an administratively subordinate position. Means of production were no longer centrally allocated. Raw materials and other materials had to be subcontracted by agreement with other enterprises. The prices and quality of goods had to be negotiated. Sale of products was guaranteed by contracts with the purchasers. Relationships among enterprises were to be established without the intermediacy of a central distributing apparatus.

The Hungarian planned economy ceased being a quantity economy, i.e., a natural economy, and prices were no longer merely units of accounting. They therefore had to be set more realistically, i.e., they had not only to cover costs but also to ensure a balance between supply and demand. Thus, the economic reformers directed their principal attention to adequate price formation. Prices were repeatedly adjusted; state subsidies were dismantled, with the aim of gradually bringing the domestic price system into line with world market prices. Also, the exchange rate of the forint was to be set more realistically, and the multiple exchange rate system replaced by a uniform exchange rate. Enterprises producing for foreign trade were thus provided with adequate parameters, and the trade earnings could be built into their internal accounting system without the intermediacy of the state budget.

An end was put to the isolation from the foreign market of enterprises producing for foreign trade. The larger among them were even granted the right to establish direct contacts with foreign clients and to assume full responsibility for foreign trade transactions. Several production enterprises obtained permission to conduct transactions with foreign firms on a commission basis, subject to the agreement of the foreign trade firm concerned. Manufacturers of export goods were therefore forced to think about costs and quality to obtain a good price on the world market. The foreign trade results, profits or losses, were no longer taken over by the state budget, but were incorporated directly into the economic accounting of the production firm. The enterprise itself, rather than the state, was to have control of its production results: profit, which in a cencentralized steering model serves only as one of many indices of efficiency, became the one important factor deciding the fate of an enterprise, and had a considerable influence on the remuneration of the enterprise management and personnel. The state continued to have a share in a firm's profits, but no longer had as much control over them as formerly. After deduction of taxes, the remaining profits were to stay with the firm: a part for development purposes, and the rest for bonuses to the enterprise management and personnel.

An essential element of the Hungarian reform of 1968 was not only the relaxation of central planning and the liberalization of administrative methods but, above all, the breaking of the "iron law" that a planned economy had to place primary emphasis on heavy industry.

The agricultural cooperatives were henceforth freed of the daily surveillance of the central authorities and were finally able to cultivate those crops for which they were best equipped and which promised the greatest return. Within a very short time the relaxation of pressure from above brought considerable improvement to Hungarian agriculture. Hungary's economy awoke from its lethargy. Enterprises, now forced to rely on their own initiative, released forces that had remained hidden to the omniscient administrative bureaucracy, namely, the creativity of the producers, now freed from their lead strings and daily surveillance, who suddenly were able to feel that their initiative meant something and that it could bring greater benefit to the enterprises and hence to themselves as well.

## THE REFORM ENCOUNTERS DIFFICULTIES

The economic reform of 1968 proceeded smoothly for four years, until 1971. The orthodox groups, who would have liked to present their own losses as a violation of the principles of Marxism-Leninism, were unable to bring the reform to a halt. This brief period was recorded as the "golden age" of Hungary's economic history. The economy and, especially, agriculture recovered, and the incomes and consumption of the population rose; the decentralization of decision-making powers and the relaxation of administrative constraints had created a totally new atmosphere, freed from pressures, in the society at large. The economic bureaucracy had lost its monopolistic power over the economy, and the intellectual bureaucracy, its power over people's thoughts. Not only the economy but the entire society could breathe more freely.

But it was just this circumstance that constituted the greatest danger to a small party elite, which had had its rights curtailed. It launched a counteroffensive. It is not true, as is generally claimed, that the reform was first brought to a standstill by the oil shock. It was the conservative party elite, dethroned by the reform, not economic constraints, that brought the creative forces to a standstill for five years. The two great pioneers of the reform, Jenö Fock and Reszsö Nyers, lost their seats in the government and the party leadership, and the other reformers were forced onto the defensive. The spirit of the reform began to erode in 1972; the oil shock of October 1973 deepened the crisis, but did not initiate it. In November 1972, the opponents of the reform carried the day in the Central Committee of the Hungarian Socialist Workers' Party. The power of the branch ministries and the central planning authorities was strengthened, and the decision-making powers of the enterprises were reduced.

The mistakes of the decentralized economy were meticulously exploited in the struggle against the reform. Weakening of the power of the central authorities also put an end to the priority economy. Those branches of heavy industry that had once received preferential treatment were showing clear signs of dissolution. More and more of the work force had shifted into other branches where the working conditions were easier. The unmistakable structural transformations that were taking place in Hungarian industry encountered the strongest resistance from the opponents of the reform. Other negative symptoms were also visible, however: glaring discrepancies between the inflated development funds of the enterprises and the availability of capital investment goods and labor were becoming more and more frequent; the decentralization of decision-making powers had shifted a large part of investment activity into the hands of the enterprises at the cost of state priority investment projects. The dispersion of capital investment funds, which had always been hostage to the planned economy, had increased considerably in recent years. The imbalance had deepened in many sectors of the economy. The government had to intervene to curb inflation: wage increases were prevented by fiscal measures, prices for important goods were set centrally more frequently than had been intended, and the injection of credits was cut back.

The price shock at the end of 1973 accelerated the erosion of the economic reform. Even a planned economy has no magic powers for absorbing rising costs other than passing them on, either directly, to production prices, or globally, by the state, to the population. The Hungarian government decided to absorb a large part of the price shock in the state budget. Domestic prices were left unchanged, and the differences between domestic and foreign prices were financed through subsidies. Decentralization of economic authority lost all meaning since the economic units no longer had control over the most important instrument of their independent activity. The state once again interceded between them and the world market. Further, the state once again assumed the function of reallocating enterprise profits. The relationship between the macro level and the micro level had reverted to the traditional channels of authority and subordination. "From the beginning of 1973 to the end of 1975, there was no more talk of the reform in official circles. But it was also not criticized. It was simply forgotten that a reform had begun in 1968."[2] The reform simply ceased functioning.

The conservative party officials took advantage of the rapidly deteriorating economic situation to eliminate the mechanisms that had been set in motion by the economic reform. The sharp rise in the price of fuels and raw materials meant that prices for Hungary's imports increased twice as rapidly as export prices. The unfavorable terms of trade not only produced a growing balance-of-trade deficit but also disrupted the economic mechanisms that had been instituted before and during the reform. Hungary's planned economy had no self-regulating mechanisms to adjust the internal price system to price developments on the world market. The exchange rate was still a conversion factor for integrating foreign trade transactions into internal accounting systems. Neither then nor now has it functioned as a monetary category that automatically links the internal price system to prices on the world market.

The way the Hungarian government responded to the unexpected difficulties clearly shows how half-heartedly the 1968 reform had been introduced. The most important economic and political institutions remained totally untouched, and under such conditions everything could return to its previous status.

And indeed this is what happened. The course of reform was too young to be able to withstand the pressure of an imported inflation and a counterreform. The traditions and mechanisms of the centrally administered economy were much older, and how to set them working again had not been forgotten. The restoration was all the easier because nothing had been changed in the central political apparatus; it was still easier for it to intervene with administrative measures than to reinforce the new economic mechanisms, which continued to be regarded as alien elements.

The standstill to which the economic reform in Hungary was brought in the years 1973–1975 shows clearly how difficult it is to attempt decentralization of an economy in a one-party regime. The party apparatus, which had undergone very little restructuring over the course of time, found it easy to keep the effects of worldwide inflation away from Hungarian enterprises by administrative means. The steering mechanisms introduced at the beginning of the economic reform rapidly degenerated under the new conditions. The decision-making powers that had been granted to the enterprises fell into disuse.

The internal price system was increasingly warped by state subsidies. In the years 1974 and 1975, subsidies for imports increased significantly: 70 percent of the price rise was financed in 1974 from the state budget. Two negative aspects became apparent in this connection: a growing budget deficit and a distortion of production prices. The subsidized prices were no longer able to function as allocation factors. More important in this context, however, was a growing divergence between state interests and enterprise interests. A first effect of this was that the salubrious intentions of the economic reform could no longer be pursued. The state budget shielded the enterprises from the effects of the world market, as it had always done in the traditional monopoly of a centrally planned economy over foreign trade and currency. The state absorbed the losses. With the aid of budget subsidies, the economic units were able to maintain their development funds, even to expand them, and to raise workers' wages and thus to increase the pressure on the internal market, at a time when it would have been in the interests of the state to freeze or cut back both investments and incomes. Instead of losses reflecting growing production costs, the economic units showed profits, which at bottom were no longer covered. A portion was used to create development funds, in accordance with the rules in force. These funds, in turn, financed investment projects, which the enterprises set up to the extent that the powers granted to them permitted. It was all the easier for the enterprises to carry through their projects because state control had been weakened in the course of the economic reform. The enterprises continued to import needed investment goods, but now more and more from the West than from the CMEA, since only the West was able to finance the gap between imports and exports through credits. A balance between imports and exports with each trading partner continued to be required in intra-CMEA trade.

It cannot be ruled out that the adjustment of domestic prices to the needs of the world market was delayed because hopes were still entertained that the gap would not be too great and would, moreover, be of short duration, and that the price rises in October 1973 would not affect Soviet oil deliveries. This, however, was a mistake, for the Soviet Union, which supported the demands of the oil-producing countries, also wanted to take advantage of the opportunity presented, including even in foreign trade with its partner countries in the CMEA. On 1 January 1975, a reform in price formation was instituted, and, as a result, oil prices doubled. Soviet prices have never been as high as world market prices, even today. The price rise, however, was sufficient to plunge Hungary, a small country dependent on imports, into a serious payments crisis. In 1975 Hungary's losses in foreign trade reached the mammoth sum of 35 billion forints, or almost $1 billion.[3] The enterprises could be shielded from the rush of inflation, but the country as a whole could not. To maintain economic growth and the accustomed level of consumption, imports were continued, and the growing foreign trade deficit was financed with Western credits.

The state, which financed the growing difference between domestic and foreign prices with budget subsidies, once again took control of the most important lever of economic management. A sense of what could be produced domestically and what could more advantageously be imported from abroad was gradually lost. The force supporting the economic reform, namely, the economic mechanisms introduced during the course of the reform, had lost its economic content. There was no other recourse left, therefore, but to strengthen state control. The Eleventh Party Congress of the Hungarian Socialist Workers' Party, in 1975, thus put principal emphasis on the central plan and control of plan fulfillment and stressed that the effectiveness of the central plan depended neither on the plan targets nor on the careful management of economic units, but on the decision-making system and on observance of the adopted resolutions.

Of course, the economic achievements in the period from 1968 to 1972 could not be attributed to the economic reform alone, nor was the abandonment of the reform wholly to blame for the later failure. In the late '60s and early '70s, the country profited from a revival of foreign trade and extremely favorable terms of trade. In 1973, however, exchange conditions took a turn for the worse. Foreign trade also meant the importation of a huge inflationary wave, with which the economy was simply unable to cope. To be sure, stronger economies were affected at that time as well. But unlike the situation in market economies, Hungarian enterprises were spared the pressures of an unfavorable trade situation. They were therefore not forced to undertake appropriate economizing measures and alter their import structure. Under the pressure of the economic difficulties that suddently set in, advocates of the economic reform very soon gave way to a counterreform. The general rules established in 1968 simply ceased being applied, as they had not yet been incorporated to any extent into the existing economic and political system. Although the reformers had defined the "new economic mechanism" as a "socialist market," no true market with self-regulatory mechanisms had emerged. The new steering instruments were not institutionalized. Political institutions had remained completely untouched, and it was continually stressed that the economic reform had nothing to do with politics. Nonetheless, Hungary's experiences have unequivocally shown that economic powers can be consistently decentralized and such an economic reform can be of lasting duration only if there is a concomitant liberalization of state power. The reversion to centralist tendencies was also made possible by the fact that the 1968 reform had created a conflict between the decentralized decision-making powers in the economy and the centralized state power.

A revival of the central plan and increased state controls were, however, unable to cure the economic problems. On the contrary, enterprises that the state had relieved of concern for the restoration of equilibrium through massive budget subsidies were also little concerned with state interests. State discipline remained ineffective. For at least three to four years, the state protected enterprises from the effects of the worldwide inflation. The negative consequences were unmistakable. The economic levers no longer functioned. The budget deficits rose considerably, and domestic prices diverged widely from the world price system. In the mid-'70s, production prices were already, on average, 2 percent higher than consumer prices.

The undermined mechanisms of a centralized economy were inadequate for overcoming the economic difficulties and restoring the shattered equilibrium. But the triumph of the counterreform was of short duration. The reformers did not give up their struggle for a liberal economic system.

## REACTIVATION OF THE TENDENCIES TOWARD REFORM

The party leadership, unwilling to liberalize the exercise of political power, took new courage under the pressure of the economic recession and the functional weakness of the traditional mechanisms of a centralized economy and reactivated the economic reform, by then almost fallen into oblivion. "Had the political decision in 1977 been different," said one of the leading protagonists of the economic reform, Csikós-Nágy, "these years could very easily have meant the end of the reform."[4] The alternative options were convincing to no one: the proposal to overcome the increasing disproportions by stimulating economic growth proved to be impracticable, since a 1 percent growth required 1.3–2 percent increase in imports, and with this, exports were unable to keep pace. Just as unrealistic, and for social reasons even dangerous, was the proposal to reduce the standard of living, already low, by 10 percent, or to raise even more credits in the West, in the hope that they sooner or later could be reduced to a bearable level by creeping inflation. In the meantime, the debt service was consuming a growing portion of the national product, and hidden inflation went to work: in 1977 the state budget allocated a 16 percent subsidy to the price of meat, 66 percent to the price of milk, 38 percent to the price of coal, and 27 percent to the price of grain. Public transportation had to be subsidized to the tune of 117 percent of the officially set fare.[5]

Developments in the '70s once more demonstrated to the party leadership that in Hungary, which is very dependent on foreign trade, a centrally managed economy no longer has any future, that a dynamic but disproportional growth at the cost of consumption does not bring social peace, and that a nation's economy can adapt and respond appropriately to international developments only if every unit in the economy experiences the impact of those developments directly, without the benefit of state subsidies. These considerations brought about a return to the basic principles of the 1968 economic reform.

## THE NEW ECONOMIC MECHANISM IS REVIVED

The basic principles remained unchanged. The novelty was that the steering methods were more closely coordinated with the goals of economic policy, and the internal price system was more radically attuned to the developments of the world market prices than before. The Eleventh Party Congress (in 1975) set up a committee whose task was to create adequate steering mechanisms to improve Hungary's competitiveness on the world market.

Even more important in this context were the adjustments made in economic policy, especially the adaptation of real economic growth to the reduced possibilities resulting from the price explosion. The guidelines of the five-year plan for 1976–1980 clearly showed that Hungary's economic policymakers realized sooner than Poland's party leadership how dangerous disproportionate economic growth, financed with expensive Western credits at the cost of consumption, could be.

Many of the targets of the five-year plan were intended to restore equilibrium to the Hungarian economy as rapidly as possible.[6]

– The national product, a parameter used domestically, was to rise more slowly than the domestic resources needed for it; the difference between the growth rates of these two economic parameters was to be conducive to the expansion of exports.

– The export-oriented development projects were to be given top priority; the Hungarian National Bank was required to create an appropriate credit fund to finance such projects.

– Foreign credits were to be used primarily to finance export-oriented investment projects.

– Domestic prices were gradually to be brought into line with the world market prices.

The decision of the October 1977 session of the Central Committee had a substantial influence on Hungary's economic growth:

> In the future, economic efficiency shall be promoted by ac-

> commodating the structure of production to the conditions of domestic and foreign markets better than heretofore; stress shall be laid on the promising branches of the economy, and less efficient sectors are to be downgraded so as to reduce pressure on scarce economic resources. The price and subsidy system shall contribute better than heretofore to the restructuring of the country's economy.[7]

The quality of produced goods was henceforth to be the principal criterion of efficiency, and only those economic activities were to be recognized as qualitative that were competitive on the world markets. The measures adopted at the October session in 1977 and the December sessions of the Central Committee in 1978 and 1979 were further elaborated in the decisions of the Twelfth Party Congress (24–27 March 1980): "Our economic policy gives due consideration both to the laws of the construction of socialism and to imperatives deriving from the country's situation as a nation."

Social ownership of the means of production and a socialist planned economy remained fundamental. "But commodity, money, and market relations are also an organic part of socialist economic life."

The Twelfth Party Congress described the principle of the resuscitated 1968 reform more precisely. The basic idea of combining central management and extensive self-sufficiency and independence for economic units into an organic whole was to be implemented on a more concrete basis than before. A key role was assigned to the central plan in the formulation of economic policy. It was not, however, to function as a binding state directive, nor were specific targets to be given to the individual enterprises; rather, economic mechanisms were to be used to fulfill the plan.

To set the economic reform into motion again, it was necessary to reorganize the economic mechanisms that had been thrown into disarray by the price explosion, especially the price system, which had been totally warped by the massive subsidies. Prices, states a Party Congress decision, must work to give a rational structure to production and consumption; production prices should be shaped to correspond to developments in the world market, to promote technical progress and improve the quality of goods, and to control the movement of retail prices.

## THE RESTRUCTURED STEERING MECHANISMS

### Prices

The price system was subjected to a thorough review. The branches of the economy were divided into two groups: economic branches that participated actively in international foreign trade, and branches that functioned only for domestic consumption. The prices of the first group were basically to be brought into line with world market prices, and, accordingly, those for fuels and raw materials with import prices on the Western market, which were still higher than the prices obtained in intra-CMEA trade. This would give consumers an incentive to use scarce resources more sparingly. Domestic prices for finished products of industrial branches participating in foreign trade were to be brought into line with prices obtained through export. In this case as well, these were the prices on Western markets, which, however, were usually lower than the prices in intra-CMEA trade.[8]

The other branches, those not participating in foreign trade, would adapt their prices to those of the exporters or set them on the basis of the prime costs of production. Certain changes were to be made in retail prices; there was a return to the former two-tier price system that had been abolished in 1975 and 1976. The general rule was that production prices were to be 10 percent lower than retail prices. The difference was to be borne by consumer prices and put into the state budget in the form of a turnover tax.

In July 1977, the largest price rise since 1946 was instituted for consumer goods. Prices for basic foodstuffs were increased by 20 percent; for meat, by 30 percent; and for bread, by 50 percent. The overall price index rose by 9.7 percent. In the first half of 1980, consumer prices increased by another 12 percent. In 1979 prices were set officially for 55 percent of consumers' goods. It was generally agreed, however, that the proportion of officially set prices would decline from 55 percent to 40 percent in the next two to three years.[9]

The adjustment of the relationship between wholesale and retail prices was intended to create conditions for establishing a uniform exchange rate. The organic relationship between a uniform exchange rate and the domestic price system was described as follows by János Fekete, vice-president of the Hungarian National Bank: 'Money is best able to fulfill its functions as a measure of value and as a means of payment and accumulation if the exchange rates in all international finance transactions, both commercial and noncommercial, are uniform. A uniform exchange rate can be instituted only if we have a suitable price and tax system."[10] On 1 October 1981, a uniform exchange rate of $1 for 35 forints came into force.

## Profitability and the distribution of profits

The price reform was intended to make enterprise profits more realistic so that they could become the leading criterion of economic efficiency. Many external, but also domestic, factors, especially the massive rise in the prices of raw materials and fuels and the 10 percent increase in agricultural products and 5 percent in transport rates, effected a rising trend in industrial prices. To counteract this trend, the 5 percent tax on means of production introduced in 1968 was abolished while, at the same time, the wages fund fee paid by enterprises was reduced from 35 percent to 17 percent.[11] The profitability tax, built into sale prices, was reduced from 15 percent of production assets to 6 percent.[12] The reduction in the profitability tax was in line with the economic policy pursued by the government of thus "reducing the discrepancy between the self-financing funds of enterprises and mitigating the more difficult conditions of expanded reproduction" (Csikós-Nágy). However, operating conditions vary from one branch of the economy to another. Therefore, the profits had to be differentiated: for the iron and steel industry and machine-tool industry, the tax was maximal, at 15 percent in 1980, whereas for light industry, it was the lowest, at 2 percent.[13]

The guidelines for the utilization of profits were also modified. The basic principle of the economic reform, that enterprises should have control over their own profits, was pivotal: taxation was increased from 36 percent to 40 percent, and the depreciation rate for building the development fund was increased from 15 percent to 25 percent. The remaining profit was used for incentive purposes. The enterprises themselves have control over both the development funds and the residual profit.

## Financing of investments

Among the most important components of the restructured steering mechanisms are the modified guidelines for decision making and the financing of investments. In view of the scarcity of resources, no taxation on investments is provided for. The volume of investments set out in the five-year plan for 1981 to 1985 is about 1,000 billion forints, i.e., 20 billion forints more than in the preceding five-year period. Greater emphasis is also to be given to investment projects initiated by the state, whose share in total investments increased from 46 percent in 1975 to 53 percent in 1980. The major projects initiated by the state are financed with bank credits and the enterprises' own funds; the sources of financing for enterprise investment projects will be the development funds, made up of profits, and bank credits; if these two sources are not sufficient, budget subsidies may also be employed, but in the form of direct grants.

## Restructuring of wages

As with investments, no rise in real wages is planned for the five-year period from 1981 to 1985. Csikós-Nágy, Chairman of the Hungarian Price Committee, has said, "The standard of living that has now been achieved can be consolidated with only a 1.5 percent annual average increase in consumption."[14] Real wages, the growth rate of which fell from a 3.3 percent yearly average for the period 1971 to 1975 to 0.7 percent in the following five-year period, from 1976 to 1980, will not be able to rise in the current five-year period; the planned increase in consumption (the targeted increase is only one-third of the growth rate achieved in the '70s) depends on a rise in the number of persons employed and on the automatic increase in fringe benefits and bonuses that are paid out in addition to wages. The wage policy follows the principle that in the period 1981 to 1985 "the remuneration received in the preceding five-year period will not be maintained; workers will have to work better for the same wage." Wages will depend more than previously on performance: the traditional, annual, centrally applied, universal 1.5 percent increase in wages has been abolished, and in the future no rise in wages will be permitted without a corresponding increase in productivity. At present a uniform wages schedule applies to all workers. The level of wages has been made dependent on both working conditions and skill. Five levels of skill have been distinguished: simple work, semiskilled work, simple skilled work, highly skilled work, and the work of a foreman.

The combination of these two evaluative criteria has produced a schedule of thirty wage levels; however, enterprise management itself is permitted to decide on the amount of wages in the specific case. Supplements of 20 percent and 30 percent are allowed for second-shift and third-shift work, respectively. Measures have been undertaken to ensure the stability of the work force: the state authorities support interfirm agreements that prohibit the hiring of a worker from another enterprise or provide for refusal to hire a job applicant who changes his job more than twice a year.

As in the other Eastern countries, in Hungary, too, the right to work is written into the constitution. Full employment at any price, however, causes considerable losses. Budapest statisticians have calculated that the performance of the 4.1 million working people is 15–20 percent below the norm (232–233 days). An average of 2.5 million working hours is lost yearly through wasted time, unexcused absence, or lack of materials. The bold attempt of the vehicle and machinery factory Rába, in February 1979, to dismiss 249 unnecessary white- and blue-collar workers has not been imitated, nor did it enjoy the approval of state officials. The anomalous situation that some firms have excess labor while others have a shortage is dealt with by permitting savings accruing through a lower number of employees to be used to raise wages.

## The convertibility of the forint

A consistent price reform intended to bring the domestic price system in line with world market prices and the readjustment of the exchange rate thus made possible were intended to create conditions for at least a limited convertibility of the forint. The president of the Hungarian National Bank, Matyas Timar, observed that this convertibility should be seen "neither as a short-term goal nor as a sweeping measure." The sole objective was to enable the forint to be used in foreign trade, the export proceeds expressed in forints to be either converted by the foreign purchaser into foreign exchange or used to buy Hungarian goods.[15]

János Fekete, vice-president of the Hungarian National Bank, observed that the goal of convertibility was in conformity both with the principle of state monopoly over foreign trade and currency in planned economies and with the principles of the comprehensive program of the CMEA of July 1971. It would, he said, promote Hungary's economic stability and increase its credit-worthiness on the world markets: "A convertible forint would be clear evidence of the stability and uninterrupted growth of the Hungarian economy and would result in a further improvement in the international reputation and credit-worthiness of Hungary." It would also, he said, be "compatible with a socialist planned economy."[16]

With its application for membership in the International Monetary Fund (IMF) and the World Bank on 5 November 1981, the Hungarian government took a further and important step toward bringing the forint into the world currency system. Hungary became a member of the IMF in June 1982.

## HUNGARY'S ECONOMIC REFORM — A TENTATIVE EVALUATION

At present Hungary's economy has the most modern steering system in the CMEA. An attempt has been made to make as extensive use as possible of the margin of freedom permitted by the social system. The success of the economic reform introduced in 1968, interrupted for the period from 1973 to 1975 and later resuscitated, is to be measured in terms not so much of the efficiency achieved as of the social peace and the degree of accommodation to domestic and external economic realities attained. It should be borne in mind, however, that the great achievements and above-average growth rates belong to the past. Interestingly, they belong to the period up to 1956, which, for good reason, is regarded as the most difficult period in Hungary's postwar history. At that time, as György Aczel, member of the Politburo of the Hungarian Socialist Workers' Party, put it, Hungary had ceased to be "a land of three million beggars; during that time fundamental social and economic injustices had been eliminated."[17] The methods of a war economy employed during that period and the terrorist regime led, however, to the October 1956 uprising. Those methods cannot be repeated. The Hungarian reformers have proposed an alternative to a centrally administered economy, and are attempting as well to put it into practice. Indeed, the economic units enjoy much more independence than in the other CMEA countries.

Nevertheless, the reform is still a great experiment, whose success is contingent on its consistent implementation. The price shock of 1973 did considerable damage to the reformist ideas, since absolutely no one knew how to cope with it and absorb it into the country's economic accounting: whether directly, i.e., as the rules introduced by the reform would have required, or as is done in a traditional steering system. But the price shock cannot be wholly blamed for economic stagnation, since the losses were covered by credits raised in the West. In the four years from 1975 to 1978, the losses in foreign trade amounted to 125 billion forints,[18] i.e., about $3.5 billion. Hungary's net indebtedness as of the end of 1979 was, according to American estimates, about $7.3 billion,[19] and according to Hungarian estimates, about 5.2 billion.[20]

The most important aspect of Hungary's economic policy is that it brought growth rates under control and absorbed the imported inflation into the accounting of the enterprises, though with some delay. In this way, conditions were created that have enabled the new economic mechanisms to be reactivated. Zero growth was decided upon, and the steering system has been made more responsive to the ups and downs of the world market. Thus, the steering model has been brought into line with the development model.

Two evaluations of the Hungarian economic reform, one thoroughly optimistic, by the London Economist, and the other, a more measured evaluation, although still thoroughly objective, by the Soviet economic expert M. Usijewicz, are worth noting. The London Economist observed: "The economic revolution now taking place in Hungary will perhaps never be completed.... Hungary will probably never become an Eastern European Austria, as many Hungarians would like (even if no one would admit this openly). But the ways in which it is endeavoring to alter its economic methods make it one of the most exciting countries of Eastern Europe."[21]

The Soviet economist M. Usijewicz writes:

> Hungary's experiences show that under certain conditions economic planning can rely upon a steering mechanism in which economic incentives can play an important role....direct links were established among enterprises; the interest of the work force in enterprise proceeds has increased; the margin for self-initiative granted to the work force has also contributed to improving the efficiency of the enterprises.

So much for the positive results of the economic reform. Usijewicz also observes, however, that the desired economic efficiency has not been achieved, that the production structure has improved but slowly, and that technical progress remains unsatisfactory. The following final observation, with which one can wholly agree, seems more important than the above-quoted statements: 'Hungary's planning system, which has existed for twelve years, has contributed to the development of positive processes in the Hungarian economy. But these experiences show clearly the limits of a steering system based on economic mechanisms and demonstrate that such a system also has no self-regulatory mechanisms."[22]

This sober evaluation of the successes and failures of the Hungarian economic reform, which, of course, need not unconditionally reflect the opinion of the Soviet party leadership, nevertheless clearly demonstrates that the limits of this reform are understood and that there is no desire to portray it as a threat to the political regime. Two prominent Hungarian economic policymakers see the preconditions for more effective and lasting reform of Hungary's economic and political system better than others: the former Prime Minister András Hegedüs sees the principal cause of Hungary's difficulties in the fact that "bureaucratic structures have developed in economic life that elude any control, even control by the party. These bureaucratic structures consume a considerable portion of our investments." In his opinion, the solution to this problem depends on "whether the political leadership can tolerate the emergence and existence of autonomous movements without which significant social reforms are inconceivable." Rezsö Nyers, a former member of the Politburo, the one who is generally referred to as the "father of the reform," believes that "The success of the newly introduced economic policy will depend on the capacity of the party leadership to draw broad layers of the population into the decision-making process." In an interview he expressed the following opinion:

> In the first years of the dictatorship of the proletariat.... we demanded no more than support for our policies....now, however, it is not enough to make central decisions consistent with the interests of the people; today we must act together with the people. The people must participate in growing measure in decisions at all levels....[23]

The danger that the party leadership might move away from the base, something that in Poland has led to a severe crisis, is seen even more clearly by Imre Somogyi, Secretary of the Central Committee: "The situation is dangerous if people in leading positions terrify those around them, use any means, and behave like barbarians." His maxim is: "The duty of a party official is to lead, not to dominate."[24]

The Hungarian economic reform will always be seen as a major attempt to go beyond the limits of a centrally administered economy, to restructure economic units into functioning enterprises, and to continue economic growth after eliminating the major disproportions so as to be able to develop the country into a modern industrial nation. Hungary's per capita income of $3,340 in 1979 was still much lower than that of the Western industrial countries. In light of the above discussion, however, it must be doubted whether a lasting and far-reaching decentralization of economic authority is possible without extensive liberalization of political power.

# 2

# East European Industrial Nations—the GDR and Czechoslovakia—with a Steering System for a Developing Country

The economically underdeveloped countries of Eastern Europe have found it easier to cope with the economic and political systems forced upon them than have those nations, such as the German Democratic Republic (GDR) and Czechoslovakia, that were already developed. The Russian experiment has demonstrated that a backward country can be industrialized even without capitalists, perhaps even more rapidly than under the conditions of a market economy, but not that a democratic and humane social system can be achieved under such conditions. The price of industrialization under noncapitalist conditions has been very high: the stage of "primitive accumulation," with an above-average investment rate, a stage the industrial nations of Western Europe and North America, and East Germany and Czechoslovakia as well, already had behind them, had to be passed through. Such a social process has no claim to universal validity — it is typical of developing countries. It can achieve more or less reasonable results if nationalization of the means of production, central planning and administration, and a one-party regime are accepted as means of overcoming backwardness. So far, no Western industrial nation has embarked on this path. The circumstances under which this Soviet social system was established in the GDR and in Czechoslovakia are well enough known.

Before World War II, East Germany and Czechoslovakia already had a developed economy on a par with that of Western Europe, and beyond the level of development that, "according to Marx," would have been ripe for a postcapitalist social system. As a consequence of the catastrophic economic crisis of the early 1930s, however, instead of a proletarian revolution, Hitler's fascism emerged victorious in Germany; and the most economically and politically developed country of Eastern Europe, Czechoslovakia, was one of its first victims. History, in fact, does not follow the scenario theoreticians imagine for it. The most educated Marxist could not have foreseen that a "proletarian revolution" would take place in a country in which the proletariat made up no more than 5 percent of the population, and that a fascist takeover would occur in a highly developed capitalist country.

The instigators of the October Revolution acted against all rational theory in attempting to establish a postcapitalist social system in a semifeudal country. It was more wrong to impose a social system designed for developing countries on industrial nations.

## THE GERMAN DEMOCRATIC REPUBLIC

### THE GDR – INITIALLY EXPLOITED

Hitler's war was a crime against humanity. The partition of Germany, a consequence of that war, is even more ridden with conflict than the conditions of the Treaty of Versailles. From the very beginning, the economic conditions were much less favorable for East Germany than for West Germany. The economic division created a largely isolated economic region in the eastern section of the country, which, though it produced "advanced goods in chemistry, motor vehicle, aircraft, and electrical engineering industries, fine mechanics, and optics, had practically no raw materials and semifinished goods to supply these industries."[1] Instead of concentrating on traditional economic sectors, East Germany, like the other Eastern countries, invested enormous funds in the basic materials industries, which in West Germany were especially highly developed.

For East Germany, the first phase of development was rendered more difficult by the fact that the losses suffered from wartime destruction, dismantlings, and reparations were much greater than in West Germany. The German Institute for Economic Research gives figures of 41 percent of industry damaged, with a figure of 33 percent for the Western zone.

The dismantlings, which hurt Germany more than they helped the occupying power, were, however, not the only, and perhaps not even the most oppressive, form of reparations: in addition, East Germany had to effect deliveries from current production, a kind of reparation that was practiced exclusively in the Eastern part of Germany. Initially these reparations were to amount to $10 billion (at 1938 world market prices). A portion was later rescinded.

Including the deliveries from the Soviet stock companies (the SAGs), they were to amount to about 15 percent of the social product in the first postwar years. It should be noted in passing that the Soviet Union invested none of its own capital in these companies. It merely transformed 200 East German major factories into SAG factories, kept them until 1953, and then returned them to the GDR (the uranium mines excepted).[2] The reconstruction period was easier for West Germany, not only because it did not have to deliver goods without payment but also because it received considerable food assistance and free deliveries of machinery and raw materials as part of the Marshall Plan and other assistance programs. The total assistance provided by the Marshall Plan amounted to $3,907 million in the period from July 1945 to December 1955.[3]

Damage Rate in Percent of Total Assets in 1939

| | Western zone | Soviet occupation zone |
|---|---|---|
| Due to wartime destruction | 21 | 15 |
| Due to dismantling | 12 | 26 |
| Total | 33 | 41 |

Source: Deutsches Institut für Wirtschaftsforschung, Handbücher DDR-Wirtschaft. P. 18.

## A REORGANIZATION OF THE ECONOMIC AND POLITICAL SYSTEM

In September 1945 the transformation of property relations was begun: farms with an arable area of more than 100 hectares plus those that had belonged to war criminals or leading National Socialists were expropriated and distributed among more than 200,000 new farmers. Somewhat later, however, both new and old property were converted into collective property.

Nationalization of the industrial means of production was initiated by the "Soviet military administration in Germany" (SMAD). A referendum carried out in mid-1946 in Saxony was to provide the juridical or legal basis for this. First, industrial enterprises whose proprietors were regarded as politically compromised were nationalized. This transferred almost 4,000 enterprises to the state and transformed 200 major enterprises into Soviet stock companies. Later, nationalization was continued by means of taxation devices; the establishment of semi-state-owned enterprises was encouraged by granting advantageous tax rates and by preferential supply of materials; in the handicrafts industry, this led to the merger of private enterprises with handicrafts production cooperatives (PGHs) and to commission agreements between private enterprises and state or cooperative trade organizations in the retail trade sector.

Collectivization of agriculture began in 1952; as a result, more than 90 percent of the arable area was combined in approximately 19,000 agricultural production cooperatives (LPGs) and state-owned farms (VEGs). Subsequent development showed how great an affinity existed between the economic and the political systems molded in the Soviet Union and transplanted later to the other Eastern countries with a war economy. Indeed, Lenin expressed a desire, just after the October Revolution, to organize the Soviet economy on the model of the German postal system or the Ludendorff war economy. His wish was fulfilled with the transformation of the institutions of East Germany's war economy into a planned economy of the Soviet type. Many of the operating regulations issued during the war remained in force; aided by the planning authorities of the various administrative regions and the state administrations for industry, trade and supplies, etc., the Soviet military administration initially assumed the function of a central control body. In 1948, the powers of the Soviet occupying power were transferred to the German Economic Commission (DWA), founded the year before; when the GDR was established, this was converted to the "Provisional Government of the GDR."

## BRINGING INTO LINE

The transformation of the social system of East Germany began long before the partition of the country was resolved as an issue. The Communist Party, which after World War II saw itself as a single party for the whole of Germany, was not yet ready to proclaim publicly that it intended to emulate the Soviet social system in Germany. The founding task of the German Communist Party (KPD) of 11 June 1945, "contained minimal radical democratic demands rather than a wholly socialist maximum program; in any event, there was no talk of the ultimate objective of establishing a communist one-party regime."[4]

The program outlined at the time did not differ essentially from the declarations of the Eurocommunists of Italy or Spain of today; certain assets and firms, stated the program, were to be nationalized; otherwise, private initiative, based on private property, was free to flourish to its limits. The Soviet system, it asserted, was not to be imposed upon Germany. The theory of a "special German way to socialism" was maintained just as strongly as were the corresponding conceptions, at that time, in the leadership of Bulgaria, Poland, Czechoslovakia, and Hungary. The ideological spokesman of the Communist Party, Ackermann, declared that the proletarian dictatorship of Germany would achieve socialism by the peaceful means of parliamentary democracy. The Socialist United Party of Germany (SED), solemnly declared at the Unification Party Congress of the KPD and SPD of 22 April 1946, that the "present special situation of Germany offered the possibility of a democratic path toward socialism," and that the SED would resort to revolutionary means only "if the capitalist class abandons the soil of democracy."

The euphoria of the German Communists over their independence was of but short duration, though there is no reason to doubt the forthrightness of the declarations uttered at that time. The pressure from without was simply too strong. The Potsdam agreement on a new "noncapitalist and noncommunist, democratic, antifascist" Germany, proved to be just as illusory as the Yalta agreement on the democratic structure to be given to the other Eastern countries.

The prominent Soviet ideologue Boris Ponamarev declared in 1974 that it had been the goal of Soviet diplomacy up to 1957 to create an alliance between the two German states within an independent bloc-free confederation.[5] In reality, however, Stalin had already determined the fate of Germany in 1948. In light of the fait accompli in the Soviet occupation zone, the partition of Germany was unavoidable. The German way to socialism ended "as in the other Eastern countries, each embarking upon the only possible path, namely, the Soviet path," which, as the former advocate of independence Ackermann stressed, "did not have to be exactly the same, or on the order of a complete analogy." Once the GDR was founded, in 1949, there was no more departing from the Soviet way to socialism. At the second party conference, in 1952, the SED declared its unequivocal allegiance to the "leader of nations, the great Stalin," and with good reason, too, since Stalin had had a decisive influence on molding the leadership of the Communist Party of Germany: of 23 KPD leaders of the Weimar period who had died a violent death, 4 were murdered before 1943, 8 were murdered by Hitler, and 10 were murdered by Stalin.[6] The world public learned of this after the Twentieth Party Congress of the CPSU in 1956.

Within the SED there was no longer any deviation from the general line: potential opponents were reprimanded promptly — Merker and Guber in 1950; Schirdewan, Wollweber, and others in 1958. No death sentences were pronounced in the GDR, however. In West Germany, on the other hand, the KPD lost most of its members. In the first local and regional elections in 1946, it was still able to gain 9 percent of the votes, but in the Bundestag elections of 1949, its percentage was 5.7, and in 1953, it was no more than 2.2 percent. The successor to the KPD, the German Communist Party (DKP), has never had more than 50,000 members.

## AMBITIOUS ECONOMIC PLANS, THE JUNE UPRISING, AND THE BERLIN WALL

The economic aims established by the party leadership were too ambitious to be achieved. It was simply not possible to do everything at once: to drive full steam ahead with reconstruction, to make good the burdensome reparations, and to supply the population with food — moreover, under conditions that required a readjustment to totally new supply and sales markets and, in addition, to a steering system unsuited for an industrial state. As in every planned economy, the needs of the population were at the bottom of the list of priorities. It was realized too late that the considerable lag behind the standard of living of West Germany, which became greater rather than smaller with time, would inevitably lead to an unending population drain if the borders were kept open. The most highly skilled preferred to flee from socialism back to capitalism: in 1946 the population in East Germany (18.49 million) was still higher than in 1939 (16.74 million); as a result of the influx of immigrants, it increased to 19.1 million in 1947; but by 1961, when the Berlin wall was built, it had fallen to 17.08 million.[7]

According to the evaluative criteria of a planned economy, the first five-year plan (1951–1955) was a tremendous success: national income increased by 85.3 percent. The population measured the successes and failures of the government in other terms, however, namely, in the rise in the standard of living. In these terms, the first postwar years were much more difficult for the East German than for the West German population. Because of the wide dispersion of investment projects and the special impetus given to the investment goods, the purchasing power of the population increased considerably, but the supply of foods and other consumer goods did not. A considerable portion of current output had to be used for reparations.

As in any planned economy, the GDR government found only one means of fighting inflation: increasing work norms, which softened the rise of wages. The response of the workers was the mass uprising of 17 June 1953. Soviet tanks were used, and law and order were restored. The deep gap between the ambitious, but disproportional, notions of growth held by the government and the demands of the population for a higher standard of living could not be bridged, neither then nor now.

The second five-year plan, from 1955 to 1960, was intended to eliminate the disproportions that had been created in the first half of the '50s: a long-term "chemistry" program was spelled out in 1958, and a number of enterprises and whole branches of industries were to be nationalized as part of a program of "socialist reconstruction."

Importance was also attached to eliminating difficulties in supply after the June uprising. The "new course" obligated industrial enterprises to produce additional consumer goods; discontinuation of deliveries from current production to the Soviet Union was also intended to ease the situation somewhat. The consumer goods industry did not, however, move upward on the list of priorities.

In 1959, the five-year plan was abandoned. It had had no chance of success: in the five-year period from 1956 to 1960, economic growth was 41.1 percent, compared with 85.3 percent in the preceding five-year period.

Walter Ulbricht took his inspiration from Khrushchev's plan to "overtake and pass the United States within the historically shortest period." Just as in the Soviet Union at the time, a seven-year plan was also drawn up in the GDR; the aim was to bring the GDR up to the standard of living of West Germany by 1961.

The "principal economic task" proved to be unrealistic. Instead of rising, the growth rate fell, from 11 percent in 1959 to 6 percent in 1960 and 4 percent in 1961. At the end of the '50s, the population's consumption was 25–30 percent below that in the Federal Republic[8]; the flow of emigrants increased. On 13 August 1961, the Berlin wall was built. The purpose of this wall, which in the official language of the GDR is called an "antifascist wall of defense," is clear: all efforts to achieve the standard of living in West Germany had failed; to curtail the growing flow of emigrants, the GDR had to seal itself off hermetically.

## A NEW ECONOMIC SYSTEM WAS PLANNED, BUT THE OLD REMAINED

The men in power in East Germany understood quite well that it was the steering system that had condemned them to backwardness. There was a willingness to reform it slightly, but not to such an extent that it would come into conflict with the one-party regime. At the Sixth Party Congress of the SED (January 1963), it was resolved to institute the "new economic system of planning and management."

The experience with a centrally administered economy had clearly shown that this was not a suitable system for a highly developed country like Germany. The problem, after all, was not, as in other Eastern countries, to create the preconditions for the transformation from an agricultural country to an industrial economy. Concentration of power as a means of centralizing resources so as to develop heavy industry was superfluous in the GDR since its industrialization period was far behind. A centralization of decision-making powers might have been useful in a country in which the managerial stratum was still very modest, but not in the GDR, which had a large potential of managers and technologists.

The GDR has always operated under its capacity and, in addition, has wasted costly materials and raw materials that have had to be imported. Using gross output as the principal criterion of economic success had inevitably led to waste and, moreover, in just those areas where economizing was at a premium. The unreal if stable prices of a planned economy neither provided any indication of scarcity of resources nor were informative allocation parameters. Overcentralization of decision-making was intolerable especially because it reduced the interest, initiative, and personal responsibility of managers and staff to a minimum.

There were therefore many reasons to reform the steering model, which did not fit the conditions of an industrial society. Walter Ulbricht was a great party *apparatchik* of the Stalinist type, but no reformer of a social system. If the reformed steering model was referred to as "the new economic system" and, since 1967, as "the economic system of socialism," it was not because a qualitatively new system had been introduced, but because of the desire to mask the paltry content with a fine-sounding name.

The reform system was doomed to failure from the outset because it saw the law of human activity for society in a sense contrary to human nature. Walter Ulbricht saw the relationship between the individual and the general interest differently from Adam Smith. At the Ninth Central Committee Meeting of the SED in October 1968 he formulated the link between the enterprises and the economy as a whole, a link that was the crucial factor in efficiency, as follows:

> Planning the economy as a whole is to be thoroughly and precisely linked to the economic accounting of state-owned enterprises so as to stimulate the initiative of enterprises and employees and steer them as precisely as possible in a direction that accords with the interests of the society, of enterprises, and the interests of the working people.[9]

This formulation reflects a fundamental contradiction between a planned and a market economy: in a planned economy, the intention is to bring the personal interests of the individual into line with the overall interests of the state by means of the subjective decisions of the political leadership; in a market economy, on the other hand, the overall good is the sum of individual achievements brought into line with the whole by means of authentic and tested mechanisms. No planned economy has yet been able to shape the instruments of planning and administration at its disposal in such a way as to optimize satisfaction of the needs of the individual.

The GDR was also unable to create, with its new economic system, a mechanism capable of bringing the interests of enterprises and their staffs into line with the overall interest. A command economy had therefore to be re-created.

The main contents of the "guidelines for the new economic system" of 11 July 1963 were to redirect central planning toward long-term goals and to reduce the binding target figures to a minimum; indirect steering by means of economically based prices and monetary instruments (economic levers) were supposed to replace, at least partially, the administrative steering instruments. The margin of decision-making powers of an enterprise was to be expanded considerably; the principal responsibility for economic achievement was shifted to the associations of state-owned enterprises (VEBs), which were transformed from purely administrative agencies into "bodies of economic leadership" and were subject to the principle of economic accounting. Prices were to serve as objective parameters for assessment and allocation; the gross plant assets at mid-year in 1963 were reassessed on the basis of the replacement prices of 1962; the depreciation rates were set high, and prices covering the costs were introduced in three stages.

An important component of the new economic system was the reorganization of the banking system. The planned-economy banking network was replaced by a banking structure with market features. Business operations were separated from the functions of the central bank, which had to operate as the "bankers' bank." Since 1968, the State Bank of the GDR has had to keep accounts for the state budget and the commercial banks, in addition to issuing currency and controlling foreign exchange. The GDR Bank for Industry and Trade, on the other hand, assumed the functions of commercial banks; the Agricultural, Foreign Trade, and Cooperative banks and the savings banks assumed their respective specialized functions. The investments of enterprises were henceforth to be financed from profits, depreciation, and bank credits, instead of nonrepayable funds from the state budget, as formerly.

In contrast to the original provisions governing the foreign trade monopoly, export firms would have henceforth to cope with conditions on the world market to a greater extent than before, and the profits and losses from foreign trade were to be included in the overall firm results.

The "economic system of socialism" was destined to be short-lived. It failed because of its own intrinsic inconsistency. The state hierarchy guarded its power jealously, and would not willingly permit anonymous market forces to take the place of its arbitrary decisions. Firm managers, on the other hand, who had become accustomed to having everything handed to them and to working for 100 percent certain markets, were also not eager to make the change to more independent responsibility. The new steering system within the old structures had never drawn a clear boundary between the decision-making powers of the state-owned enterprises, their associations, and the various sectoral ministries. Even this minor shift of power to the microlevel jeopardized the fulfillment of centrally set economic targets. Thus, the party leadership quite early, in 1968, found itself compelled to initiate "product-linked planning," in which priority was given to the production of goods important to the state and, on the supply side, to raw materials, other materials, and labor. The disproportionalities that were supposed to have been eliminated by the recently introduced mechanism grew even greater. The "economic" mechanisms, onwhich so much hope had been placed, were increasingly absorbed by the traditional structures of a planned economy, and lost the modest economic attributes that had been expected of them. Prices did not move in accordance with the costs of production; they did not even reflect a scarcity in production factors. Under these conditions, the new market-modified banking system also lost any economic meaning. The idea of integrating the results of banking operations into the results of the economy as a whole by means of a refinancing system was never put into practice because the state continued to determine the credit volume as well as prices and interest rates. On 1 July 1974, the market-modified banking system was abolished, and the traditional planned-economy structure was restored.

The growing imbalance was also the reason for the reversion later to more rigorous state management and state supervision in foreign trade as well. The government resolution of 1 December 1970 restored exact planning of exports on a quarterly basis; the rules governing the allocation of foreign exchange for imports were tightened perceptibly. At the end of the '60s, unfavorable climatic conditions made the economic situation, already critical, even graver. Acute bottlenecks sprang up in the energy sector, accompanied by further troubles in a number of other areas of the economy, such as agriculture, construction, transport, etc. Accordingly, the Central Committee of the SED (meeting of September 1970) decided on even greater centralization; the number of binding indicators was increased, and the competence of the enterprises was drastically curtailed.

The "economic system of socialism" had ceased to function, without having been officially abolished. One had become poorer in illusions, and richer in experience: if economic mechanisms are not an integral part of a real market, but rather the state itself determining their function, sooner or later the state will discard them. The state hierarchy is not so keen on giving up the power to administer the economy as it sees fit, and shares its power with the power of the "invisible hand" of the market very unwillingly.

The centrally administered economy had to cut down the economic mechanism to manageable size, and reactivated the command functions of the central authorities. The status quo ante was restored. But this steering model, which had already proved unsuitable for the earlier stage of development, proved to be even less suited for the later phase of an industrial society. The developments of the '70s were an emphatic confirmation of this.

## QUANTITATIVE GROWTH AT THE EXPENSE OF QUALITY

The GDR is the most advanced industrial nation of the Eastern bloc. In terms of economic potential, it ranks among the top ten nations of the world. In terms of real per capita income, however, it ranks among the top twenty. The GDR is no longer capable of generating new impulses conducive to progress in the Eastern bloc.

To be sure, the quality of life of the population in the GDR is much better, and supply difficulties are much more manageable than in the Soviet Union, Poland, or Romania. But it must be asked why it is that in the GDR, which covers a territory half as large as the Federal Republic of Germany, has no more than 21.6 percent of the total population of the two Germanies, and has a level of employment (53 percent) much higher than West Germany's (42 percent), supply difficulties nevertheless occur — why, for example, ham and salami are scarce items; why the waiting time for Trabant and Wartburg cars is seven to ten years; why the society is divided into those who possess premium D marks, for which premium goods can be purchased in the Intershops, and those who have low-premium GDR marks, for which there is no guarantee that what one needs can always be purchased. The answer seems to be unambiguously clear: the GDR is an industrial nation whose economy is managed with the mechanisms of a developing country. Thus, investment projects and investment goods have top priority, and mass consumption is of secondary importance.

The GDR state usurps the power to make decisions. Even though some powers have been delegated to firm management, the reins of administration are never permitted to become so loose as to enable the independent initiative and creativity of the individual to develop adequately; the centrally set economic targets have priority. The manager in a planned economy is a faceless, anonymous, state administrator who deals with plan targets, not with the requirements of the market. Indeed, the plan may even be fulfilled to the letter, yet bring no major benefit to the society.

In this relatively highly developed industrial nation, quantity is still the dominating concept, the notorious "ton" ideology, which persists despite numerous attempts to eradicate it. The categories of value are meant more for the accountant than for the firm manager. Prices remain unchanged for years on end. They did not even respond to the price shock of 1973 until the end of the decade, and then as a consequence of state command. Inflation gaps are closed by state subsidies. Though profit, interest rates, and similar mechanisms play a greater role than formerly, this playing around with "economic mechanisms" is still no more than "walking on eggs with unreal prices."

In foreign trade, a "foreign-exchange mark" is used. Though what it entails may be known to statisticians, bank officials, and economic experts, it has scarcely any meaning for exporting or importing firms. The GDR does not have a convertible currency, or an exchange rate based on economic realities, because these value categories are incompatible with a command economy. A currency confined to domestic needs can be adequate only in an autarkic economy, but not in the East German industrial economy, which must import raw materials and fuels and export finished products. A nonconvertible currency reduces any country that engages in foreign trade to the level of a developing country, regardless of its economic strength.

## THE SEVENTIES WERE TO HAVE BEEN A PERIOD OF CONSOLIDATION

After the economic growth of the '60s, which was more impetuous than balanced, steered initially by the "new economic system" and then, later, at the end of the decade, by the traditional centrally administered system, the '70s were to be a period of consolidation and balance. A somewhat lower growth rate than in the second half of the '60s was deemed an acceptable price to pay for evening out the imbalances that had arisen — especially the balance-of-payments deficit in foreign trade — or at least to reduce them.

The growth rate of the GDR in the second half of the '70s was 22 percent, which was 8 percentage points less than in the first half and 5.3 percentage points less than the plan target. Industrial goods production also increased more slowly (28 percent) than in the preceding five-year period (37 percent). Although the growth rates were more modest and the plan target was not achieved, the GDR could still boast of a relatively good growth in the most important branches of industry in the second half of the '70s — and this despite the Soviet Union's having considerably raised its prices for crude oil, gas, and coal.

Indicators of Economic Growth in the '70s
(Average Annual Changes, in Percent)

| | 1971–1975 | 1976–1980 | |
|---|---|---|---|
| | Actual | Plan | Actual |
| Produced national income | 5.5 | 5.0 | 4.1 |
| Industrial goods production | 6.7 | 6.0 | 4.7 |
| Labor productivity | 5.2 | 5.4 | 4.7 |
| Output in construction | 5.7 | 5.0 | 4.5 |
| Finished housing units (in thousands) | 122.0 | 150.0 | 163.0 |
| Agriculture | | | |
| Gross product | 2.3 | 3.6–4.5 | 0.4 |
| Retail trade turnover | 5.0 | 4.0 | 4.1 |
| Imports | 14.1 | | 10.3 |
| Exports | 12.8 | | 10.2 |
| Capital investments | 4.1 | 5.2 | 4.8 |

Sources: Statistisches Jahrbuch der DDR 1979; Wochenbericht des Deutschen Institutes für Wirtschaftsforschung, 6/81 and 31/81.

The price increases for crude oil and the reduction in the delivery quotas by the Soviet Union had the greatest impact on the chemical industry, which saw a decline in its annual growth rate from 8.3 percent in the first half of the decade to 4.7 percent in the second half. The energy and fuels industry was more dynamic, with an average growth rate of 4.6 percent, compared with 3.1 percent in the preceding five-year period. The growth rates declined, however, from 7.0 percent to 3.8 percent in metallurgy, from 6.8 percent to 2.6 percent in the construction materials industry, and above all, in those sectors aimed at the consumer: from 6.7 percent to 4.2 percent in light industry, and from 5.9 percent to 2.4 percent in the foodstuffs industry.

The GDR discovered, somewhat too late, that the age of microelectronics had arrived. The decision of the Sixth Session of the Central Committee of the SED in 1977 stressed the economic importance of this sector and the need to accelerate its development. Since then, however, electronics and electrical engineering have advanced to the leading positions in economic development: with an average growth rate of 8.7 percent, they could boast of the highest growth rate in the second half of the '70s; in the first half-year of 1981, the growth rate was even 10.9 percent.

Stagnation set in in agriculture. The annual growth rate was, on average, no more than 0.4 percent in the second half of the decade, compared with 2.3 percent in the preceding five-year period; the growth in net income of the population and in retail trade turnover decreased from 27 percent in the five-year period 1971–1975 to 19.8 percent for 1976–1980 and from 28 percent to 22 percent respectively.

Capital investment in the GDR has shown gaps similar to those in the other East European countries. Although the investments increased at a lower rate than in neighboring Eastern countries, with a growth of 28 percent in the second half of the '70s, they expanded 7 percentage points more slowly than in the first half of the decade; per capita, the GDR invested 4,160 marks (in 1977, according to calculations of the German Institute for Economic Research), almost as high a figure as in the Federal Republic (4,240 marks). However, productivity was only half as high. Whereas between 1960 and 1976 the Federal Republic invested 3,200 marks to increase the social product by 1,000 marks, the GDR had to invest almost twice as much, i.e., 6,200 marks, to achieve the same increase.[10]

The low capital productivity is a consequence of the typical dispersion of investment projects in a planned economy. The construction time is much longer than in market economies. Ingo Wolf, scholar at the Academy for Social Sciences, attached to the Central Committee of the SED, writes: "As long as the construction time is in some cases as much as double the internationally usual time, high scientific and technical performance is economically unattainable."[11] The number of incompleted investment projects is higher than average. In April 1979, Erich Honecker announced before the Central Committee of the SED that investment projects had to be examined "project by project" for their urgency. For 1980, the number of projects was reduced from 450 to 250. In addition, "incompleted investment projects" were thenceforth to be included in the statistics. The purpose of this inventory was to reduce the completion times and, where possible, to make unused machinery available to other firms. Similar measures to control the excessive capital investment ambitions of firm managers had been undertaken in the past without success, however, because state-subsidized investment projects were the cheapest means of fulfilling and overfulfilling plan targets.

The GDR economy was not consolidated in the '70s. This was not because of excessive disproportions in the respective growth rates of individual sectors of production or because the lag behind West Germany that was to have been made up by the beginning of the '60s had become smaller, but because the accomplishments of the '70s were achieved at the expense of an enormous debt to the West.

## A FOURTH OF ALL GDR EXPORTS WHICH GO TO THE WEST ABSORBS ALMOST 90 PERCENT OF THE TOTAL BALANCE

The GDR has an intensive share in the international division of labor, with exports making up 20 percent of the national product in 1980. Foreign trade showed a vigorous growth in the last five-year period, as is evident from the following table.

GDR Foreign Trade in the Period 1976–1980, in Billions of Foreign-Exchange Marks

| | 1976 | 1977 | 1978 | 1979 | 1980 |
|---|---|---|---|---|---|
| GDR imports | 45.92 | 49.88 | 50.71 | 56.43 | 62.97 |
| GDR exports | 39.54 | 41.84 | 46.17 | 52.42 | 57.13 |
| Total | - 6.38 | - 8.04 | - 4.54 | - 4.00 | - 5.84 |

Source: Wochenbericht des Deutschen Institutes für Wirtschaftsforschung 31/81.

Note: One foreign-exchange mark in 1980 = 0.597 DM.

The CMEA countries had the lion's share of foreign trade in 1980: 60.2 percent of imports and 65.4 percent of exports. The figures for the Western industrial countries[12] were 30.5 percent of imports and 24.1 percent of exports. The Soviet Union was the leading trading partner of the GDR, making up 36 percent of its total foreign trade. A distant second was Czechoslovakia (9.2 percent), followed by Poland (8.3 percent), the Federal Republic (6.3 percent), and Hungary (6.2 percent).[13]

The Federal Republic of Germany was first among the Western trading partners of the GDR, with 62.5 percent of exports and 57 percent of imports; the United States was a distant second (imports 9.8 percent, exports 0.9 percent), followed by France (5.6 percent and 5.3 percent) and Austria (4.0 percent and 3.2 percent).[14] It is noteworthy that the GDR, which conducts two-thirds of its foreign trade with the CMEA countries and felt the impact of the oil price shock especially acutely in its relations with the Soviet Union, has accumulated an enormous foreign trade deficit, particularly in trade with the Western countries. Since the beginning of the price rises in fuels and raw materials, the GDR balance of trade has shown a chronic deficit. In the five-year period from 1976 to 1980 alone, it was about 17 billion DM; the greater proportion of the debt, about 15 billion DM, has been accrued in trade with the Western industrial countries, Austria accounting for 365 million DM (2,601 million shillings). The foreign trade deficit with regard to the Soviet Union, the main supplier of fuels and raw materials for the GDR, has risen to 5.4 billion DM in the last five years.

The principal reason for the deficits are the unfavorable terms of trade; the cumulative trade deficit in relations with the Soviet Union corresponds almost exactly to the increased price for crude oil. Nevertheless, it cannot be said with certainty that the GDR is a net debtor of the Soviet Union since the GDR participates on a credit basis in "joint investment ventures," mainly on Soviet territory, which between 1976 and 1980 accounted for 8 billion GDR marks.[15]

The credits granted to the Soviet Union will eventually be covered by oil and gas deliveries; the existing trade deficit must continually be reduced, however.

The foreign trade deficit with the industrial nations of the West is financed by short-term and long-term credits raised in the partner countries and on the Euromarket. The deficit to the Soviet Union (9.06 billion foreign-exchange marks in the five-year period 1976–1980) has been reduced, by multilateral clearing mechanisms of the International Bank for Economic Cooperation, to 4.2 billion foreign-exchange marks, and the remainder has been financed with clearing credits from this bank.

GDR Debt to the Industrial Countries of the West (in Millions of Dollars)

| | 1971 | 1975 | 1976 | 1977 | 1978 | 1979 | 1980 |
|---|---|---|---|---|---|---|---|
| Gross debt | 1.408 | 5.188 | 5.856 | 7.145 | 8.894 | 10.140 | |
| Net debt | 1.205 | 3.548 | 5.047 | 6.159 | 7.548 | 8.440 | 10.0* |

Source: National Foreign Assessment Center, Estimating Soviet and East European Hard-Currency Debt. Washington, D.C., June 1980.

*Estimates of the Deutsches Institut für Wirtschaftsforschung, Wochenbericht 31/81.

## THE DEBT SERVICE BURDEN

The GDR debt of $503 per capita at the end of 1979 was only 10 percent lower than the per capita debt of Poland. However, the ratio of the debt and debt service of the GDR to its exports was considerably lower:

| | Ratio of debt to foreign exchange earnings (in percent) | | Ratio of debt service to foreign exchange earnings (in percent) | |
|---|---|---|---|---|
| | 1972 | 1979 | 1972 | 1979 |
| GDR | 95 | 223 | 18 | 54 |
| Poland | 87 | 333 | 15 | 92 |

Source: Ibid.

Although the above indicators for the debt burden are much more favorable for the GDR than for Poland, the debt service is more than twice as high as the generally accepted limit (25 percent).[16]

The GDR economy was unable to overcome the price shock and to square its balance of trade. In the last five years, much more was distributed than was produced. The gap was about $17 billion, which is 19 percent of the gross national product of $89.1 billion.[17] The debt service is too great a burden. As a rule, new credits are raised to pay back those that have come due. Only $171 million of the $2,646 million of credits raised in 1979 were for capital transfer. Interest payments are most oppressive: between 1976 and 1979 they amounted to $2,585 million, $1,075 million in 1979 alone.[18]

The Federal Republic is not only the leading trading partner of the GDR but also its leading creditor. The cumulative debt was 3.9 billion DM at the end of 1980; most of this is financed commercially, only one-fifth being financed through the "swing," set at 850 million DM. Despite many years of effort, the GDR has not been able to achieve any major sales successes in the Federal Republic, especially in the area of machinery deliveries. Hence, the FRG must deal continually with the problem of consenting to accept products from other sectors, especially foodstuffs and industrial consumer goods. It should be noted that only once in the past decade, in 1980, was the GDR able to achieve a positive balance of trade of 285 million DM in internal German trade.[19] Trade with West Germany is of major importance for the GDR, not only because a considerable portion of the negative balance is financed with the interest-free swing credit facility but also because it is not subject to customs. It has, however, lost some of its momentum: in the first half-year of 1981, deliveries to the GDR increased by only 6 percent, while exports from the GDR increased by 3 percent.[20]

One of the leading creditors of East Germany after the FRG is Austria. The gross debt increased from 7.5 billion shillings in 1976 to 16.0 billion shillings in 1980; GDR exports to Austria in 1980 were no more than 2.1 billion shillings. The ratio of debts to exports (1:7.6) is thus more than three times as great as in credit relations of the GDR with the other Western countries.

The GDR entered the '80s with a considerable debt and an uneven balance of trade. It had not yet overcome the price shock, and thus seems to have little prospects of being able to eliminate its foreign trade deficit in the near future. Hence there are no sources other than new credits for repaying interest and credits that have fallen due. Furthermore, the GDR is unable to cut back on imports, because the production capacity created in the last decade is both energy intensive and material intensive. In contrast to Poland, the GDR does not have exportable goods such as hard coal, sulfur, and copper. There are always, however, major difficulties attendant on imports from Poland. Accordingly, the GDR leadership has been following developments in this neighboring country with growing attention. In terms of percentage, Poland has the same share in East German foreign trade as does the GDR in Polish foreign trade. But Poland has always been an important supplier of coal and coke, and if exports of these goods stop, they cannot easily be replaced: in 1979 the GDR imported 1,925,000 tons of coal, or 22.1 percent of its total requirements, from Poland, and 457,000 tons of coke-coal (15.4 percent). But the 4,456,000 tons of coal (52.8 percent of total requirements) imported from the Soviet Union also came mostly from Poland. At the end of April 1981, however, Poland had supplied no more than 14.3 percent of the annual quota to the GDR, compared with 22 percent during the same period in the preceding year.[21] Poland also supplies 19.6 percent of GDR total imports of electrical engineering equipment; 80 percent of GDR transit trade to the Soviet Union passes through Poland.

## THE "ECONOMIC STRATEGY OF THE EIGHTIES"

Ambitious growth targets were established: the national income was to increase by a yearly average of 5.1–5.4 percent in the five-year period from 1981 to 1985 (the actual growth in the preceding five-year period was 4.1 percent), and industrial goods output was to increase by 5.1–5.4 percent a year (the actual figure for the preceding five-year period was 5.0 percent).

Once again, however, the priorities for some of the sectors on which progress was contingent were politically motivated. Priority was given to the preferences of the central planners rather than to those of the consumer. Special stress was placed on electrical engineering and electronic products. These sectors of the economy had the highest growth rates (9 percent) of all industrial sectors. The machine tool industry received the same consideration: its annual growth was planned at 7 percent, to contribute to the planned export offensive. The above-average growth rates in the chemical industry were, however, a thing of the past. Although this industry was supposed to perform important tasks for the economy as a whole, such as process more crude oil and boost the carbon chemical industry on the basis of brown coal, the cutback in oil imports meant an average growth rate of only 6 percent. The unfavorable prospects for hard coal and oil imports have forced the GDR leadership to increase the country's utilization of domestic brown coal. Whereas in preceding years the mining of brown coal was kept, as a matter of principle, at the same level of 250 million tons, by 1985 a volume of 285 to 290 million tons is planned. Despite this high backlog demand, an average growth rate of about 4.7 percent to 5.1 percent yearly is targeted for light industry. The unfavorable prospects for agriculture have been more realistically evaluated. In the preceding five-year period, agricultural production increased by an average of 0.4 percent a year; for the five-year period from 1981 to 1985, no more than a minimal annual increase of 2.0 percent to 2.2 percent is expected, animal production increasing 0.9 percent to 1.0 percent. It is simply not possible to meet the growing needs for fodder through imports.

In view of the fact that major importance is attached to increasing foreign trade (the foreign trade turnover is to increase by 36 percent from 1981 to 1985), targets for the increase in income have had to be more modest, namely, an annual growth rate of 4 percent. The same growth rate has been targeted for retail trade turnover, stress being placed not so much on volume of high-quality consumer goods as on the increased value of turnover in the broad network of "Exquisite" and "Delicate" shops, in which prices have risen exorbitantly. The prices for basic foodstuffs continue to be subsidized: subsidies for 1981 are projected at about 20 billion GDR marks.

The intention is to achieve these ambitious plan targets not only by means of a rather modest growth in consumption but also through minimal capital investment expenditure, which is to increase by only 1.8 percent to 2.3 percent annually. The GDR economy cannot hope for any considerable increase in its labor force; the number of employed will increase by only 235,000 persons, compared with 310,000 in the preceding five-year period.

However, the creaking steering system will be the greatest obstacle. Whereas Walter Ulbricht initiated the structural transformations of the '60s with a "new economic system," Erich Honecker began the "consolidation of industry" in the '70s with a reactivated central administration system, but failed to attain it. The structural transformation that is the objective of the '80s (major stress being laid on the most advanced sectors of industry) are to be achieved with a new "planning procedure" within the existing anachronistic administrative system. Honecker can hardly expect any real capital import, and will have to reduce the mountain of debt that was accumulated during the consolidation phase. It must therefore be doubted whether Günter Mittag, the Politburo member responsible for economic affairs, is right in saying: "The formulation of the ten key points of economic strategy of our party for the 1980s, presented by Comrade Erich Honecker at the Tenth Party Congress, is part of the most significant theoretical achievements of our party today." It must also be doubted whether the SED, as Mittag thinks, possesses "a coherent conception, based on the universal laws of socialism and the experiences of a policy that has proven itself over the years for organizing the advances of the '80s."[22] The party leadership started the economic plan for 1981 to 1985 with an enormous mountain of debt and no means available for reducing it.

## THE NEW PLANNING SYSTEM[23]

The "Regulations for the Planning System of the GDR National Economy for 1981 to 1985," which came into force in February 1980, is, to be sure, an important step forward in refining planning practices, which had indeed always been better in the GDR than elsewhere. The regulations attach great value to the "conceptual preparation of the five-year plan" and to the precise planning of science and technology and, moreover, adds more binding indicators to the plan.

The conceptual preparation of the five-year plan will take place at three levels, including: (1) long-term development models, established by the Council of Ministers. At present, these concern development of microelectronics, the use of industrial robots, electronic control of machinery, the use of computers, processing metallurgy and coal processing; (2) long-term development models for a number of "crucial sectors"; and (3) long-term territorial development models for the districts, selected large cities, and regions.

The planning of science and technology will be more rigorously compartmentalized, and the crucial areas will be more clearly delimited and more centralized than before. Special importance is attached to "state commissions," which are intended to produce essential structural transformations in the economy or to have a certain breadth in their effect, e.g., planning of the products and the uses of microelectronics. More importance will also be attached to the planning of rationalization processes. A "long-term strategic model for rationalizing the nation's economy" is being considered that will be developed by the state planning commission over at least a five-year period.

Major importance is attached to the planning of demand-oriented production; in this context, industry and the consumer goods domestic trade will be jointly working out product ranges for a one-year period or longer. The list of state plan targets has been expanded. In particular, there are plan targets for rationalization as well as for science and technology. Indicators of "final product" (sale of industrial commodity output minus delivery) and materials costs per 100 marks of commodity production have been introduced.

Walter Ulbricht and Erich Honecker have done everything to refine and perfect the existing steering system, but nothing to replace bureaucratic socialism with an enlightened socialism. As the prominent theoretician of the Italian Communist Party, Lucio Lombardo Radice, put it, the existing steering system is "the Procrustean bed of further development."[24]

## CZECHOSLOVAKIA

### AN INDUSTRIAL ECONOMY IN CONFLICT WITH THE LIMITS IMPOSED UPON IT BY THE SYSTEM

Before World War II, Czechoslovakia, like East Germany, had an industrial economy comparable with that of the other industrial countries of Western Europe: with a per capita national income of $103 in 1938, Czechoslovakia ranked second among the countries of southern and eastern Europe, behind the eastern part of Germany ($189), followed at some distance by Hungary ($63), Poland ($62), Bulgaria ($43), and Romania ($38).[1] With a population of 14 million, Czechoslovakia accounted for 1.28 percent of the world's industrial potential, followed by Poland whose share was only 0.82 percent, although its population was 32 million.[2] The share of industry in the total product was already 58 percent, whereas in Hungary and Poland it was only 44 percent, in Romania, 40 percent, and in Bulgaria, 34 percent.

In the period between the wars, the industries of Czechoslovakia and East Germany were already at a "respectable European level," as the Polish CMEA expert Pawel Bożyk put it.[3] Already at that time Czechoslovakia had a highly developed metal and machinery industry; the technical level was considerable, and productivity was among the highest in Europe. Czechoslovakian railroad cars, locomotives, aircraft, and electrical products competed successfully in the most ambitious markets of the world. Its textile and shoe industries (Batia) led the field in Europe; the productivity of agriculture was above average. Czechoslovakia also had a greater share in world trade than the other Eastern countries. Its share in world exports in 1938 was 1.6 percent, whereas that of the USSR was only 1.3 percent, of Poland, 0.9 percent, of Hungary and Romania, 0.7 percent each, and of Bulgaria, 0.3 percent; 72 percent of total exports were finished products (in Poland 10 percent, in Bulgaria 4 percent, and in Romania 1 percent).

The Czechoslovakian economy suffered less from war destruction than the other Eastern countries and also was spared reparations. Czechoslovakia was the only country in Eastern Europe in which a democratic regime was established in the postwar period under two prominent politicians, Tomas Garrigue Masaryk and Eduard Beneš. There were no illegal parties. The Communist Party was legal, and the leaders of the illegal Communist Parties in Eastern Europe led the underground activities of their organizations from Prague.

A large share of the population was favorably disposed toward the social and political transformations on the horizon. Two factors were of crucial significance: the considerable strength of the Communist Party, which had been able to recruit supporters in the other parties of the country for its initially modest reform plans; and the traditionally friendly attitude toward the Soviet Union.

Although the Communist Party of Czechoslovakia celebrated the 60th anniversary of its founding on 16 May 1981, its historiography has remained incomplete, despite many efforts. However, we do know that when Czechoslovakian Social Democracy split in May 1921, Bohumil Šmeral took half of the membership, about 350,000, with him into the Communist Party, which he founded at that time. In the first parliamentary elections in which it participated as an independent party, in 1925, it won 13.2 percent of the vote. It was then the second largest party in the country. The period of its great success, however, came to an end when the left wing, under Klement Gottwald, assumed the power in the party, with his ultraleft, dogmatic, and anti-Social Democratic slogans, but above all with Stalin's help. Within a short time the number of members decreased to 25,000. Although the economic crisis of the '30s once again offered it a great opportunity, the CPČ was not able to regain the strength of its first phase. At the time of the Munich agreement, however, it still had 90,000 members.

Gottwald and his party had it easier after the war. The prewar government and the governing parties of the time were severely compromised by the Munich agreement; many politicians, especially in Slovakia, had collaborated with the Nazis. Unlike in Poland or Romania, there was no resentment of the Soviet Union in Czechoslovakia. It had not participated in the Munich agreement, and its victory over Hitler's Germany had gained it much sympathy.

Thus, the Communist Party was able, within a very short time, to gain a strong influence throughout broad strata of the population. In August 1945 it had 712,776 members (in Poland the Polish Workers Party did not have more than 235,296 members in December 1945 [4]). In the next elections, in 1946, the CPČ won 38 percent of the vote. Although the CPČ was able to triple its votes compared with the elections of 1925, and although it can be assumed that this reflected its influence within the population, we must nonetheless be somewhat circumspect in making such an assessment. A considerable proportion of the voters believed in the Košic program of 5 April 1945, which had been inspired by the Communist Party and which provided for nationalization of heavy industry, but not complete nationalization, radical agrarian reform, but not total collectivization of agriculture, and friendship with the Soviet Union, but not submission to its hegemony. Not many knew that even before the elections of 1946 Gottwald had been entertaining the idea of seizing power, by force if necessary. Indeed, he wrote: "If the unlikely should occur and we do not receive good election results, the working class and the party will find adequate means, weapons, and ways to correct the simplistic and mechanical election results, which are under the influence of saboteurs and reactionary elements. In this case as well, we will have sufficient power to drive through a result favorable to us."[5]

The Communist Party did not venture such a step in the initial phase. The reforms encountered hardly any resistance. The nationalization decree of October 1945 was implemented without difficulties, and the large enterprises, banks, and insurance companies became state property. The reforms were also supported by the noncommunist parties and by broad strata of the population. The nationalization program of Czechoslovakia of 1945 differed only slightly from the program of François Mitterand in 1981. Total nationalization of the means of production, a prerequisite for a totalitarian one-party regime, was to take place later. And no one has so clearly understood the direct relationship between a state-run economy and a monopoly of power by a state party as the democratic parties of Czechoslovakia did in this transitional phase.

Hubert Ripka, Minister of Foreign Trade in the coalition government and member of the People's Socialist Party, wrote: "Total nationalization leads inevitably to a totalitarian policy, represented by the dictatorship of one party."[6] The draft program of the People's Socialist Party states: "Humanitarian socialism is incompatible with complete nationalization of the economy, because that places all economic and political power in the hands of the state or the government."[7]

The Czechoslovakian New Economic Program (NEP), which was based on the Kosič program, was destined to be short-lived. Nonetheless, a mixed economy combined with a democratic form of government was able to survive somewhat longer than in the other Eastern countries. Before February 1948 Czechoslovakia had developed a unique steering system, which was thoroughly suited to the industrial economy of that time. Specifically, an effort was undertaken to steer a state sector, which was already quite large, and the still existing private sector with traditional market mechanisms and with non-dirigist planning, and to combine it firmly with a Western-style democracy.

This model did not fail as a consequence of poor performance; quite the contrary, it was completely successful, as was the NEP in the Soviet Union. It made possible a rapid postwar reconstruction and improved the living conditions of the population within a very short time. It was Stalin who brought the successful Czechoslovakian steering model down, because it contradicted his notion of a uniform Eastern Europe dependent on Moscow.

Czechoslovakia had no reparations to pay, but Moscow demanded so much from it that the coalition government was unwilling to meet the demands without something in return. Forced to reject Marshall Plan aid, it demanded recompense in the form of a trade agreement that would have somewhat mitigated the difficulties of the country at the time. For example, better conditions for uranium deliveries were stipulated. The Soviet Union was willing to offset the cost of production at a slight profit, but not to pay the world market price. In payment for grain, which Czechoslovakia urgently needed because of the severe harvest failures of 1947, the Russians demanded large quantities of rolled steel, part of which was resold for hard currency to the Western countries.

Gottwald risked no more free elections. In February 1948, he seized power. Soon thereafter Eduard Beneš resigned, and Klement Gottwald was "appointed" President of the Republic. Thereafter, things went in the same way as in the other Eastern countries: on 27 June 1948, he Social Democratic Party was absorbed by the CPC. Then came a total nationalization of the means of production, and shortly thereafter forced collectivization of agriculture began. The first five-year plans were worked out for 1949–1953, naturally with priorities on heavy industry, which accounted for 37 percent of all capital investments, or 5 percent more than the earlier drafts. Czechoslovakia, which even before World War II had a highly developed steel industry, began the construction of the Gottwald Foundry, which consumed huge amounts of capital for years.

Within a short time, Czechoslovakia had to thoroughly reshuffle all of its economic relations: whereas before World War II, only 11 percent of its foreign trade was with the Eastern countries, in 1949 this figure rose to 45 percent, and a year later it was as high as 60 percent.[8]

The Communist Party's monopoly on power and the total nationalization of the means of production created the conditions for the suppression of all market mechanisms. These were replaced by binding directives from the central planning authorities. In modern Czechoslovakian industrial society, the model of accelerated industrialization, with priority given to heavy industry to the neglect of the needs of the population, a model tailored to the developing countries of Eastern Europe, was put into effect. The party dictatorship, which was at variance with the country's democratic traditions, together with the model of "accelerated industrialization," which was in contradiction to the high level of development, gave rise to degenerative phenomena in economic and political life that, in the end, led to universal opposition to the regime. Police and ideological terror reached a height almost comparable with Stalin's purges of the '30s. In October 1948, the first concentration camps were set up; later they reached the considerable number of 124.[9]

The show trials and forced confessions of crimes not committed were reminiscent of Stalin's trials in the '30s. Fifty of the 97 members of the central committee of the party and 6 of the 7 members of the central committee secretariat were eliminated; 11 were sentenced to death and executed, including the Secretary General, Rudolf Slansky.

Not only the political regime but the economic system as well was fashioned after the Soviet model. The private sector was reduced to a minimum, and later liquidated entirely. Collectivization of agriculture was accelerated. After 1953, all prices were set centrally: raw materials, other materials, and investment goods were apportioned centrally, and the central planning authorities had exclusive decision-making powers over capital allocations. The Soviet model of a centrally administered economy, which did not in the least fit the developed industrial economy of Czechoslovakia, was copied faithfully.

The consequences were not long in coming. Serious difficulties cropped up in the first half of the '50s. The growth rate of the national income decreased from an annual average of about 20 percent in the period 1948–1952 to 6.4 percent in 1953 and 3.5 percent a year later.[10] Even more serious than the decline in the relatively high growth rates of the beginning period were the growing disproportions in the economic structure of the country, which especially affected the consumer. Popular discontent grew: in 1953 the Pilsner workers went out on strike; there was unrest among the students as well.

The political leadership persisted in the Stalinist style of government even after Stalin's death. Klement Gottwald survived his great benefactor by only a week. The upheavals in the neighboring countries — the 17 June 1953 rebellion in the GDR, the stormy October 1956 in Poland, and the revolution in Hungary — seem not to have affected Czechoslovakia. Four years after Khrushchev's secret report to the Twentieth Party Congress of the CPSU on Stalin's crimes, the huge statue of Stalin still dominated the horizon over the Moldau. Those who were executed in Gottwald's purges seemed to have been forgotten; those sentenced to prison remained behind bars even after their companions in suffering in their neighboring countries had long since been rehabilitated. Gottwald's successor, Antonin Novotny, liked to say: "At that time I was not among the leadership." But it was he who had prepared the charges for the Slansky trial.[11] The Novotny regime attempted to combat the often manifest inefficiency of the economy with traditional means: by tightening the reins instead of loosening them.

A far-ranging reform of the steering system was not undertaken until 1958, but even this did not touch any of the system's basic features. A certain free play was given to the microlevel in the allocation of working capital; material incentives for management and personnel were supposed to produce a rise in efficiency, and the level of the binding plan indicators was curtailed. But the central plan retained its directive character, and the central administration delegated only an insignificant portion of its decision-making powers to the enterprises.

This half-hearted, fragmentary reform created more discrepancies than it assuaged. In 1960–1961, economic growth showed another distinct decline. In 1963 the national income decreased by 1 percent. The imbalances became greater; planned coordination of the economic process seemed to be in jeopardy. The reformers ascribed the new difficulties to the half-heartedness of the reform measures, while the advocates of a hard course ascribed them to the liberalization of the steering system, which in their opinion had gone too far.

The intellectuals, who for a long time had supported the regime because of fear and opportunism, now refused to obey. Criticism became increasingly louder, and the gap between the ruling elite and the people deepened. A survey carried out in October 1968 showed that only 3 percent of those questioned identified with the regime; 20 percent described the '50s as the most unhappy period in the history of the country, exceeded only by the Nazi occupation and the period after the defeat on White Mountain (1620).[12]

## EIGHT MONTHS OF THE "PRAGUE SPRING"

Many informative books and articles have been written about the events in Czechoslovakia in the fateful year 1968, about the events leading up to it, and about its consequences. We shall deal with only a few aspects of it here: the relationship between the political and the economic reforms, those unique and extraordinary features of it that could not be fit into the geopolitical framework, the restoration of the old system and its impact on the further development of the country.

On 5 January 1968, the day on which the head of the state and the party, Antonin Novotny, resigned his post as First Secretary of the Communist Party and was replaced by the Slovakian CP head Alexander Dubček, marked a turning point in this development. The change of power was not coincidental. Fifteen years after Stalin's death, the country's leadership had been trying to maintain the regime, already discredited, with half-hearted measures. But the revelations about Stalin's crimes were not without their influence on events in Czechoslovakia.

Alexander Dubček was by no means a revolutionary. During his time in office as First Party Secretary of Slovakia, no revolutionary ideas were to be discerned in him. He maintained good relations with the Soviet Union, where he had spent his childhood. The Soviet leadership had nothing against the change of power, and Dubček's election to First Party Secretary was certainly less unwelcome to the Soviet Union than that of Gomulka in 1956. Dubček, however, had qualities that were disturbing for the party apparatchiks in all the Eastern countries. He was open and responded to the voice of the people, and was accustomed to levying hard criticism against bureaucratic monstrosities; in addition, he was extremely modest, and had maintained an ideal notion of socialism that, within the party apparatus, had long since lost any relationship to practice.

If Dubček and his followers left their mark on an entire epoch of Czechoslovakian history, indeed on world history, within a short period, this was due not only to the revolutionary and original ideas they resolved to implement but also to the personal qualities of the new party leader whom the rebellious intellectual elite of the country had appointed the executor of their demands. What was special in the "Prague Spring" was the consensus, for the first time in the history of Eastern Europe, between the ruled and the rulers, a belief on the part of both that given the right geopolitical conditions, it was possible to make "socialism with a human face" a reality. As Dubček said, he had "come to the realization that if there was no consensus between party and people, it was the party that had to change, because the people cannot be replaced by another."[13] In this respect the Prague Spring differs considerably from the developments in Poland in 1980–1981, in which the party leadership, cut off from the people, attempted to bring the mass movement under its control and impose the "leading role of the party" upon it, but succeeded only in deepening the gap between itself and the people.

Thus, it happened that Czechoslovakia, which had copied the Stalinist model most faithfully, came to manifest a unique consensus in the struggle against the sorry consequences of bureaucratic absolutism for the economy and for the cultural life of the country. Even more paradoxical was the fact that the protagonists of the renewal were those who themselves had contributed to establishing the Stalinist model of rule. As the political scientist Peter Hruby has expressed it, "After they had helped destroy a democratic system, the same people were faced with the much more difficult problem of liberalizing and democratizing the totalitarian system they themselves had created."[14]

The mass movement that the faithful Communist Alexander Dubček was to lead was against the entire social system, which, it was suddenly discovered, had nothing in common with the democratic traditions of the Czechoslovakian people. All aspects of the authoritarian regime were rejected by the people. The inadequate economic system, the failure of the half-hearted attempts to get it moving, the bitter feeling that the once-flourishing economy of the country had lost all the momentum that could have made it competitive again on the world market, as it had been in the period between the two world wars — all these things together were the decisive factor. It was poor consolation that Czechoslovakia was still in first place in the CMEA sellers' market.

A few years before his fall, Novotny had already been compelled, under pressure of public opinion, to contemplate a new economic reform. In the mid-'60s, a team was formed to work out suitable proposals. But the very first step showed that the authoritarian Novotny regime offered no conditions for a liberalization of the economic system and that the planned measures would be no more successful than those of 1958. Preparation of the draft plan began in the last quarter of 1963, the first important changes took place in 1967, but real progress was not achieved until after Dubček came into office.

The principles of the introduced reform may be summed up as follows[15]: The state plan defines the general direction of economic policy and no longer serves as an instrument of direct control; it coordinates economic activities and provides the necessary information; the market and its mechanisms regulate both internal economic relations and economic relations with foreign countries; condtions are to be created for coordinating the interests of enterprises with the interests of society; the economic units decide on production, technology, and the choice of business partners; thus, they have the necessary decision-making powers; means of production are not centrally allocated; relationships among enterprises are regulated by agreement; the state relinquishes its previous function of redistributing the financial funds of the enterprises; the latter pay taxes to the state and no longer receive state subsidies; they have independent control over their net profits.

The preconditions for implementing the above and other reform measures were first created by the action program the party leadership adopted under Alexander Dubček in April 1968. In it the Communist Party committed itself not to intervene directly in the internal affairs of the economic units; the enterprises were to be given unrestricted autonomy and were no longer subordinated to the ministries or any other central body; they were to have the right to determine their organizational structure themselves; the economic activities of medium-sized and small enterprises, which had had a sorry existence in the centrally administered economy, without any reliable supplies of means of production, were reevaluated; the workers' councils were to have a say in appointing plant managers.

The new price system was to be an important component of the reform. Three price categories were envisioned:

(a) centrally set prices for 15 percent of the turnover of investment goods and for about 75 percent of the turnover of consumer goods;

(b) free prices for 5 percent of investment and 20 percent of consumer goods;

(c) controlled prices for 80 percent of investment goods.[16]

The reform was given a revolutionary touch by a contemplated change in property relations. Most enterprises were to be "public property," were to function independently of state bodies, and be managed by factory councils; a certain number of enterprises were to remain state property and be steered directly by the ministries, which have also to appoint the majority of the factory councils; a relatively small group of enterprises would be subsidiaries of other enterprises or associations.

Differences of opinion were much greater with regard to the structure of the economy than to other aspects of the reform program. If this project had been implemented, Czechoslovakia would have had an original and quite novel economic system.

Neither the contemplated forms of property nor other aspects of the reform program became a reality. The reasons are quite familiar. Paradoxically, the draft of the "enterprise law" was not published until spring 1969, i.e., just after the invasion. Those in power had succumbed to the illusion that they could keep the entire economic reform alive even under the new conditions. Dubček and his team had continued to hope, even after the Moscow Protocol of 27 August 1968, that they could salvage at least some elements of the reform if the old leadership remained in office.[17] But the old leadership did not remain in office very long. The restoration of the old system liquidated the entire reform program.

The radical democratic movement of 1968 did not fail as a result of internal obstacles, even though, perhaps, the reform proposals had not been sufficiently weighed or handled pragmatically enough. If even today we have no proof that a "socialism with a human face," realized by Communists, is possible, it is, among other reasons, because the great Czechoslovakian experiment was not allowed to mature; the tanks that crushed the Prague Spring demonstrated that under the existing geopolitical conditions, no other socialism than the "real socialism" of Soviet cast was possible.

The reformers were reprimanded for not taking sufficient account of realities: "There was too little understanding of politics as the art of the possible," as one of the party leaders of the time, Zdenek Mlynář, put it. The question still to be answered is what specific reform projects brought the tanks into the streets of Prague on 21 August 1968. Today we are richer by one more experience, namely, the Polish experiences of August 1980. The answer seems to be that the geopolitical factor comes into play when the mass movement gets out of control, when the pluralistic forces of the people, long suppressed, are activated and push for decisions that seem dangerous to those in power in Moscow.

What the Soviet leadership fears, is certainly not that a reform movement will restore capitalism anywhere in Eastern Europe, i.e., that the means of production might once again become private property, but rather that the means of production might be converted from state property to social property, and that an authentic workers' movement might succeed in achieving what the October Revolution promised but never realized. It fears that the power of the ruling bureaucracies might be replaced by an authentic popular power, and "real socialism" of Soviet cast by genuine socialism. Such developments seem dangerous because they might be contagious and because, in Moscow, the principle holds that the "real socialism" of Soviet stamp that rules in small countries is a guarantee of the cohesiveness of the Eastern bloc.

## THE RESTORATION OF THE OLD SYSTEM HAS NOT SOLVED THE ECONOMIC PROBLEMS

The head of the planning board and Vice Prime Minister of the government put into power after August 1968, Václav Hůla, stated: "Under no circumstances do we want to return to the old, obsolete system of management"; but he then went on to add, "We cannot, and will not, tolerate that the guiding principles of management of a socialist economy should be forgotten."[18] Developments since 1968 have once again clearly demonstrated how intimately state property and an authoritarian regime are linked with central and administrative management of the economy. The "guiding principles of management of a socialist economy," stressed by the planning chief, meant, in Gustav Husák's authoritarian regime, nothing more than a new edition, if somewhat more refined, of the traditional planning and administrative practices of the Gottwald and Novotny era. The restoration of the old system also restored the essential features of the traditional economic system. Any divergences were of only a technical and organizational nature.

Peace and order within the old social-political conditions were unable to eliminate the difficulties the reform movement had created. The Soviet steering system, which had never fit the level of development of Czechoslovakia, was even less suited for an industrial state in the age of electronics and computer technology. In 1938 the per capita gross national product of Czechoslovakia was 240 percent greater than that of Bulgaria; in 1979, however, it was only 66 percent greater.[19] The reduction in the gap between the most backward and the most highly developed country of Eastern Europe after East Germany was less a consequence of the above-average progress made in Bulgaria than of Czechoslovakia's lagging behind the countries of Western Europe with which it had been approximately on a par before World War II; in 1979 the per capita income of Czechoslovakia was no more than 47.5 percent that of France, 40.6 percent that of the GDR, and 55 percent that of Austria,[20] to which Czechoslovakia had been superior before the war.

To be sure, the growth rates in Czechoslovakia are today still greater than in the industrial countries of the West. The planned economies have always been superior to the market economies in terms of quantitative growth rates. But they were, and are, inferior to them in quality and productivity. When Czechoslovakia returned to the old steering methods, it had to accept this intrinsic handicap, along with a very sluggishly rising living standard of the population, into the bargain. In the five-year period from 1976 to 1980, the average income increased by only 1.9 percent a year.[21] In 1979, wages and salaries decreased by 0.8 percent in real terms. The average income (2,640 1980 crowns[22]) was no longer more than 47 percent of the average income of an employed person in Austria (14,628 shillings[23]). Over the long term, no country can permit itself the luxury of allowing wages to increase more rapidly than efficiency; in Czechoslovakia, as indeed in any planned economy, however, salaries and wages increased more slowly than the national product. The difference from Austria is therefore greater in the case of wages than in the case of the national product. At a meeting of the Central Committee in December 1979, the planning head explained the disproportion between wages and productivity: 'Earlier it was often the case that the level of work norms was set in accordance with the desired wage." This method can hardly promote labor productivity.

If one analyzes economic development in the '70s, one sees that the margin for a rise in wages and salaries is small. They not only are much lower than in the industrial countries of the West but also rise more slowly. The average growth rate increased in the first half of the '70s to 6 percent, compared with 5.3 percent in the second half of the '60s, but in the second half of the '70s, fell to 3 percent; for the five-year period 1981–1985, an annual growth rate of 3.2–3.5 percent is planned.

Productivity, however, increased even more slowly: the growth rate of total productivity, measured in terms of the ratio of the output to the expenditure of labor and capital, declined from a 4 percent annual average in the first half of the '70s to 1.9 percent in the second half.[24]

At a meeting of the Central Committee in December 1979, party chief and head of state Gustav Husák said: "Deliveries are not even sure in terms of the time, the range, and the quality. Everyone has primarily his own interests in view and no understanding of the problems he causes elsewhere, especially for consumers."[25] Egoism is surely no less in a market economy than it is in the Czechoslovakian planned economy. The egoism of an enterprise in a market economy is, however, corrected by market mechanisms. The optimum that each enterprise may achieve through its economic egoism cumulatively adds up to the optimum for the economy of the entire nation, as Adam Smith once noted. The egoism of a state enterprise, which is tied down by innumerable bureaucratic rules, has other consequences. It is motivated by the directives of the state plan and higher levels in the hierarchy and by the rules of promotion built into the steering system. The market, which is usually a sellers' market without competition, makes no demands and does not compel maximum performance. Hence, egoism has consequences different from those in a market economy. A large enterprise that receives preferential treatment in the economic policy of a country acquires more means of production than it needs to fulfill the plan targets; this is, of course, at the cost of other enterprises, ergo of the economy as a whole. It therefore does not contribute to increasing efficiency, but rather results in higher costs and a greater expenditure of labor and capital.

Czechoslovakia, like all other planned economies, is no longer capable of achieving high growth rates by increasing its investment and labor. Raw materials have become scarcer and more expensive, and the low productivity can no longer be compensated for by an above-average labor input. Agriculture, which formerly was a reserve source of labor for industry, is itself suffering from an acute labor shortage. The average annual growth rate of the national product decreased from 6.9 percent in the five-year period from 1966 to 1970 to 5.5 percent and 3.7 percent in the two following five-year periods, respectively. Industrial output decreased from 6.7 percent in the ten-year period 1965–1974 to 4.4 percent in the second half of the '70s, and agricultural output decreased from 4.2 percent to 2.7 percent and 1.8 percent respectively.[26]

In addition to the rising costs of scarcer resources, increasing waste is another cause of the perceptible decline in economic growth. In its latest report on the world economic situation, the Economic Commission for Europe noted: "Czechoslovakia has the highest per capita consumption of iron and steel in the world; it uses about 30 percent more metal per unit of industrial output than other industrial countries."[27] The planned economy has always been a quantity-based economy par excellence. More material input has meant a greater gross volume of output, and hence also created better conditions for fulfilling the plan.

The underestimation of cost-benefit analyses is especially visible in investment activities. The level of investments is also above average in Czechoslovakia. The consequences may be seen in the exaggerated dispersion of investment projects and the enormous number of ventures that are incomplete. The limited construction capacities are continually being overstrained. In the first half-year of 1981 three-quarters of the construction enterprises of the country did not achieve their plan targets. In an editorial in the party newspaper,[28] this was called the "worst result since the beginning of socialist construction." The annual growth of investments in the five-year period 1976–1980 was only 3.4 percent instead of the 5.5 percent that had been planned.

The results of investment activities in the five-year period just ended — 30,000 incompleted industrial projects, encompassing 8,000 at over 2 billion crowns per project[29] — is hence extremely unsatisfactory. Only 50 percent of projects were completed on time; one-third were completed with a delay of more than a year. The full scope of the waste may be seen in the value of the incompleted investments, which reached 525 billion crowns at the end of 1980.[30] This immobilized value accounts for 21 percent of the total value of the country's fund of fixed assets. The discrepancy between capital expenditure and the industrial output achieved with it is steadily becoming greater: in 1970 the value of fixed assets increased by 7 percent, but industrial production increased by only 3.7 percent. In 1980 the figures were 8 percent and 3 percent, respectively.[31] The number of completed housing units is also decreasing: in 1975, 90,768 dwellings were completed, but in 1979 the figure was only 79,168, and in the first half-year of 1981, it was 16,928.[32]

Yielding to the pressure of scarcity of resources, Czechoslovakia opted for zero growth in investments in the five-year period 1981–1985, letting them stagnate at the 1980 level. Stress was to be placed on modernization, not on new construction projects. The reorientation toward rationalization measures will probably be just as ineffective in Czechoslovakia as in the other planned economies. The enterprises will, of course, not undertake the risk associated with modernization of production. A reduction in incomplete investment projects from the current 525 billion crowns to 400 billion, as targeted in the plan, therefore has little chance of success.

## CZECHOSLOVAKIA'S FOREIGN DEBT IS LOW

One point in favor in Czechoslovakia's economic policy is that it has not sought to overcome the growing difficulties, especially in the investment sector, by raising credits in the West to the extent that the other Eastern countries have done. The deficit in trade with the West ($4.9 billion in the decade from 1971 to 1980) is less than half of the trade deficit of the GDR ($11 billion) and only 28.3 percent of that of Poland.[33] The debt to the West did, however, increase considerably in the '70s: from $160 million (net) at the end of 1971 to $3,070 million in 1979. Nonetheless, it is still the lowest in the entire CMEA: it is $660 million lower than Bulgaria's debt and is only 14.6 percent of Poland's debt and 38 percent of that of the GDR.[34]

The cumulative foreign trade deficit to the West of the '70s ($4.9 billion) is, however, considerably higher than the debt to the Soviet Union (541 million rubles, or $830 million); it must be taken into account that the share of OECD countries in Czechoslovakia's foreign trade (21.8 percent of exports and 24.4 percent of imports) is considerably lower than the share of the Soviet Union (31.7 percent and 30.3 percent, respectively[35]). The share of the OECD countries in Czech exports (21.8 percent) is, after Bulgaria (20.3 percent), the lowest in Eastern Europe (average OECD share in 1980: 29.7 percent).

Czechoslovakia has considerably cut back its foreign trade with Western countries, despite the fact that it had been very active in Western markets in the period between the wars. Exports to the West in 1980 were even 3.3 percent lower than those of Romania, 42 percent lower than those of the GDR, and only 15 percent higher than those of Hungary.[36] The Federal Republic of Germany is the most important trading partner of Czechoslovakia, accounting for 35.2 percent of Czech exports to the West and 37.8 percent of Czech imports from the West. followed by Austria (15.1 percent and 10 percent, respectively).[37]

Czechoslovakia's position on the international market has declined considerably in comparison with the period between the wars. This is attributable largely to the low quality of finished products (the share of machinery in exports to the FRG is no more than 12 percent[38]), although inadequate trading mechanisms are also partly responsible. Czechoslovakia, which before World War II had a convertible currency, must now cope with a currency that cannot be used in foreign trade. Since 1954 it has ceased to be a member of the Bretton Woods institutions, although it was one of the founding members. It does not even have a uniform exchange rate. A thorough cost-benefit analysis of foreign trade transactions is made extremely difficult for this reason, and a multitude of enterprises are cut off from foreign markets by intermediate agencies.

The foreign trade deficit is a consequence of the deteriorated terms of trade (by 6 percent in the period 1973 to 1975 and 9 percent between 1975 and 1979)[39] and of the inability to achieve self-sufficiency, which has long been a goal, in agricultural products. Instead of reducing its grain imports, Czechoslovakia has had to increase them considerably in the last decade: in the period from 1950 to 1975, the annual average was 1.2 million tons, but from 1970 to 1980, it was 1.6 million tons.[40]

Although Czechoslovakia has recently been able to reduce its foreign trade deficit by cutting back on imports (in 1980, exports increased by 17.8 percent whereas imports increased by only 4.5 percent), restrictions on imports from the West will hardly be conducive to continued industrial growth over the long term. To become competitive on the world market, Czechoslovakia needs high-quality modern know-how, which at one time it was able to produce itself, but which it must now import from the West. An alternative to the import of technology would be to increase the efficiency of the domestic economy, since Czechoslovakia does, after all, still have highly skilled engineers, and the great managerial traditions of the prewar period have not yet wholly disappeared. A precondition for this would be modernization of the steering system. The state leadership knows quite well that the current system is inadequate, but wishes to avoid, at any price, a movement such as was set off by the reform efforts of 1968.

## REFINEMENT OF THE STEERING SYSTEM, BUT NO PROSPECTS FOR ECONOMIC REFORMS

At present, calm and order reign in Czechoslovakia. The party and the government control all that happens in the social, cultural, and economic life of the country. Czechs and Slovaks have a relatively tolerable standard of living; the population is relatively well provided for, even if high prices must be paid for high-quality goods (for example, two years' wages for a domestic automobile, and even four years' wages for an imported car). Since the expulsion of half a million party members who took part in the reform movement of 1968, the power structure seems again to have consolidated; opposition is reduced to a small circle of dissidents. However, the links between the party leadership and the people have weakened considerably. Many say that they are even weaker than during the time of Gottwald and Novotny. The mass media, controlled entirely by the state, have little influence on the thinking and behavior of the population. Material incentives to increase labor productivity are slight because of extensive leveling off of incomes, and there are no moral incentives to speak of. These circumstances are hardly favorable conditions for creative achievements.

To be sure, the country's leadership has no more ambitions to climb into the ranks of the pace-setting nations of the world economy; but under present political and social conditions, the Czechoslovakian economy is not even able to achieve the modest aims of "continuous growth." There are neither sufficient financing funds to expand investment activities, incentives to promote labor productivity, nor, finally, means to raise the living standard of the population, which is much too low for an industrial society.

Although the nation's economy is still expanding, if more slowly, the country is today economically worse off than at the time of the reforms of 1958, and much worse off than in the years before the "Prague Spring." The difficulties have become greater because the factors of extensive economic growth have been exhausted, and raw materials and fuels have become scarcer and more expensive. People have adapted to the Husák regime and have learned to take advantage of the holes in the authoritarianly administered economy to improve their modest incomes.

Those who restored the traditional steering system seldom criticize their own work. Those in power do not dare to initiate an effective reform of the steering system. They fear that this might revive the demands for social and political liberalization and democratization. Hence, the desire is not to alter the ailing system, but merely to modify some of its constituents in order to free new dynamic forces. The aim is to salvage what can still be salvaged under the given conditions by improving the practices of planning and administration and refining the organizational structure of the economy.

The binding character of the state plan is being left intact, even though stress has been laid on long-term planning. Thus, the main lines of the minireform introduced in 1978 have been defined. The economy is to continue to be administered by the central Party and state apparatus. No essential decentralization of economic powers is envisaged; only competences of secondary importance are delegated to the microlevel. There is no such thing as an independent enterprise that can decide for itself the direction of its growth and assume total responsibility for its decisions. As in the GDR and the Soviet Union, decision-making powers are granted to industrial associations rather than to enterprises.

Indeed, the term *economic reform* is not used, since the basic principles of the existing steering system are not questioned. In its decision of March 1980, the central committee of the party and the government merely introduced a few measures to "improve planning and steering of the economy beyond 1980." As always on such occasions, the state planning indices have been reexamined. Once again, as already several times in the past, an attempt has been made to eliminate the infamous "ton ideology": the indicator "gross output" has been replaced by the indicator "net output." Let it be noted that this indicator will hardly prevent a deft enterprise manager from fulfilling the plan conveniently for himself, but not for the state. By slightly restructuring the range of products in favor of higher price values, which does not necessarily mean a higher quality of goods, the plan can be rather effortlessly fulfilled. Of course, fulfilling the plan target of "net output" in this way is not without its negative effects. But in this case it is the consumer, not the state, who suffers.

The stress on "gross output" meant that 25 percent of processed metal was waste, that only 70 percent of lumber instead of a normal 90 percent was used productively. The target of the preceding five-year plan, to save 2.5 percent in material expenditure, was only 20 percent achieved. In the five-year period from 1981 to 1985, economizing will affect fuels and raw materials especially.

All the components of the earlier reforms are discernible in the newly introduced measures as well. However, they have been adapted to the traditional steering system, which, indeed, from the outset, was unsuited to the Czechoslovakian industrial economy. The share of an industrial enterprise in its profits is to increase from

22–28 percent to 30–37 percent, but the central planning authorities will still decide on the most important investment projects. Some though has been given to participation of the workers in plant management. This, however, is intended primarily to enable higher plan targets to be set than are stipulated in the state plan. The sum of the parts does not make for a qualitatively new economic system and creates no new impulses to promote efficiency. This conclusion is based on the experience of 150 chosen industrial enterprises, 9 trade organizations, and 21 research institutes that, since the beginning of 1978, were to test the introduced improvements in planning practice. One may read in the press that efficiency has hardly improved even since new planning techniques were introduced. Nonetheless, the new methods were introduced in other economic units as well in early 1981.

Czechoslovakia entered the '80s with an antiquated steering system that corresponded neither to traditions nor to the country's level of development. The economic problems that must be solved have become more severe. Calm and order reign in the country, but this is not enough to bring about an economic upswing. The economy and the social life of the country are stagnating. Czechoslovakian industrial society is now being steered by an economic system that is more backward than that of Hungary, which is much less developed than Czechoslovakia.

There can be no doubt, however, that both the motives and the social forces that prompted the radical democratic movement in the second half of the '60s still exist and, if conditions are right, can be revived.

# 3

# Bulgaria's Planned Economy in Harmony and in Conflict with the Soviet Model

It should be stressed at the outset that Bulgaria's planned economy, which suffers from the same contradictions as the other planned economies in Eastern Europe, has had better experiences with this economic system. Before World War II, Bulgaria was the most backward country in Eastern Europe: its share in the world's industrial output (0.11 percent in 1938) was only a third that of Hungary,[1] which had a 20 percent smaller population. The per capita national income was no more than $43, $20 less than that of Hungary and $19 less than that of Poland.[2] The rural population accounted for 79 percent of the total population, and agriculture accounted for 66 percent of total production.[3] In 1938 industry accounted for only 15 percent of the national income, and three-fourths of industrial output was consumer goods and foodstuffs. Only 4 percent of total exports were industrial products. In 1979, on the other hand, the per capita national income of Bulgaria was $3,630, i.e., only 42 percent less than that of the GDR.[4] (In 1938, the per capita income ratio between these two countries was 1:11.[5]) The share of industry in national income increased from 15 to 56.5 percent, and the share of agriculture declined to 18.6 percent.

Bulgaria has made considerable advances in the technologically advanced branches of industry: 11 percent of industrial output and 15 percent of exports came from the electrical engineering and electronics industries. This once economically underdeveloped country is currently cooperating with the other CMEA countries to develop computers. The progress this entails is not lessened by the fact that the model is the obsolete IBM system 360. Bulgaria has been able to install two of these models in India. This Balkan country has also had some notable successes in the production of lifting and conveyor machinery: every fourth surface conveyor in the world bears the trademark of the Bulgarian manufacturer "Balkan-car," which is represented in more than 40 countries, in which it sells trucks, trailers, semitrailers, and cable and chain electric lifts.

Bulgaria's dynamic development, especially during the first phase, seems to confirm the general opinion that a planned economy in the grips of a one-party regime offers a developing country better chances of growth than it does an already developed industrial society. Indeed, Bulgaria's approaching the economic level of the GDR has been due not only to the dynamic growth of Bulgaria but also to the lag of East Germany behind West Germany: whereas before the war 30 percent of the national income was produced on what is today the territory of the GDR, where at that time 28 percent of Germany's population lived,[6] the per capita income of the GDR in 1979 was only 43 percent of the per capita income of the Federal Republic.[7]

Given the underdeveloped economic and social structure of Bulgaria, in which both capitalism and the proletariat were in only rudimentary stages, it was clear from the outset that the goal of the new social order could not be the construction of a utopian socialism, but just the creation of preconditions for breaking out of the mold of a developing country. The view of one expert on Eastern Europe applies to Bulgaria even more than to the Soviet Union: "Here industrialization was not to lead to socialism, as Marx had put it; rather, socialism was to produce industrialization. Instead of being the outcome of an objective process, socialism became its precondition."[8]

This point seems also to be confirmed by the fact that Bulgaria's planned economy has, in its most recent phases, been encountering difficulties similar to those encountered in the rest of Eastern Europe.

As a developing country, it was easier for Bulgaria to make the transition to a collectivist social order than it was for the economically advanced countries of Eastern Europe, particularly because the means of production, which were scheduled to be nationalized, were still rather insignificant. Most of the enterprises that were nationalized, by government decision in December 1947, fell into the same category as those that became state property in France as well after World War II. Unfortunately, in Bulgaria small crafts enterprises were also nationalized, to the great detriment of economic efficiency and quality of life. Within a very brief period after the government decision, the state sector increased from 6 percent to 92 percent.

In agriculture also the restructurings were carried out without any particular difficulty and much more rapidly than in the other Eastern countries. It was easier for Bulgaria than for Poland, since the agrarian reform carried out in the early '20s had essentially eliminated the large landowners. The government decree of 1947, which reduced land ownership to a maximum of 20 hectares, affected only 3 percent of the total arable area of 7.8 million hectares.[9] Even before the war, Bulgaria's agriculture featured various forms of cooperation. Collectivization of the peasant holdings therefore encountered much less resistance than elsewhere in Eastern Europe. By 1950, 44 percent of the tilled surface area had been nationalized or collectivized. In Czechoslovakia the figure at that time was only 25 percent; in Hungary, 19 percent; and in Romania and Poland, 12 percent. Peasant expropriation was completed in 1958, with 92 percent of the land nationalized. At that time 77 percent had been collectivized in Czechoslovakia, 51 percent in Romania, and only 23 percent in Hungary.[10]

The political preconditions for the social system established after World War II were more favorable in Bulgaria than elsewhere in Eastern Europe. To be sure, the Soviet Union was able to give greater emphasis to its "liberating action" of 9 September 1944 than it had a month previously in Romania, since it declared war on the Balkan nation the evening before Bulgaria went over to the side of the Allies; the Communist Party was considerably stronger in Bulgaria than in the other East European countries with the exception of Czechoslovakia. The Communist Party had played a notable role in the period between the wars. In the elections of 1919, it put up one-fifth of all members of the parliament, and during its legal period was one of the two most influential parties of the country. In 1921 it counted 37,000 members.[11] In its illegal period, under the cover name of the "Independent Workers Party," it was able to win 31 of a total of 274 seats in the parliamentary elections of 1931. Georgij Dimitrov, later Secretary General of the Comintern, gave Bulgaria experienced leadership. At the time the "front of the fatherland," dominated by the Communist Party, seized power in September 1944, the party had 25,000 members[12] and was able to play an important role in the coalition government. It held the post of minister of the interior, which led a great purge of the state apparatus. In the parliament elected on 27 October 1946, only 99 delegates of the total of 465 did not belong to the "front of the fatherland."[13]

On 7 November 1946, Georgij Dimitrov became Prime Minister, and soon thereafter the social system was progressively adapted to the Soviet model. This process affected above all the influential Peasants Party, with whose aid the Communist Party, led by Dimitrov, had carried off a rebellion in 1923 against the royal government. The peasant leader Nikola Petkov was executed in September 1947. With the incorporation of the rest of the Social Democratic Party on 11 August 1948, the monopoly position of the Communists and the one-party regime were definitively secured.

The monopolistic power structures and the nationalized means of production constituted the preconditions for a centrally planned and centrally administered economy. The first five-year plan began in 1949. Heavy industry received 36 percent of investment expenditures. Thereafter the economic policies of this small Balkan country, which in the prewar period had accumulated considerable experience in the specialization of agriculture, was to be oriented toward such gigantic projects. Like the Nova Huta in Poland, the Gottwald Steelworks in Czechoslovakia, and the Stalin Steelworks in Hungary, Bulgaria began the mammoth Dimitrov Steelworks. The country's economy, which in 1937 had conducted only 12 percent of its foreign trade with the Soviet Union and the other Eastern countries, was almost wholly integrated within the Eastern bloc in only a few years: in 1948, 74 percent of Bulgarian foreign trade was with the Eastern countries, a figure that increased in the next 3 years to 82 percent, 88 percent, and 92 percent, respectively.[14]

## GOOD MEMORIES OF RUSSIA

As in Yugoslavia, the social and political transformations in Bulgaria met with acceptance among broad strata of the population. The relationship to Russia and the Soviet Union was a positive factor. Czarist Russia is still present today in the center of Sofia. A monument to the Czar Alexander II commemorates Russia's participation in Bulgaria's liberation from Turkish rule. The Alexander Nevskii Cathedral, built at the turn of the century in honor of the 200,000 fallen Russian soldiers, is the most impressive religious building in the center of the city. The Bulgarians have never forgotten that they have the Russians to thank for the independence of their country, through the Agreement of San Stefano in 1878.

The arrival of the Soviet Army in September 1944 was seen as a liberation from the hated rule of the Czar Boris III. Nevertheless, the new state leadership, under G. Dimitrov, never had the intention of copying the state system of the Soviet Union exactly. In September 1946, Dimitrov declared that Bulgaria would become "not a Soviet republic, but a people's republic, in which the functions of government would be exercised by the overwhelming majority of the people, the workers, peasants, craftsmen, and the national intelligentsia"; this republic was not to be a form of dictatorship of the proletariat.[15] At that time Dimitrov, like Tito, advocated the formation of a Balkan federation. In an interview of 23 January 1948, Dimitrov spoke of a federation that would include not only the Balkan countries but also Poland, Czechoslovakia, and, if the Communists should emerge victorious, Greece as well. Unfortunately, nothing came of this plan. Tito's and Dimitrov's paths soon diverged again: Tito continued his courageous struggle for Yugoslavia's independence and took his country out of the Soviet sphere of influence. Georgij Dimitrov, who had been sentenced to death twice, in 1923 and 1926, and who had defied the mighty Reichsmarschall Hermann Göring in 1933 in the Leipzig trial with exemplary heroism, did not dare to defy Stalin.

Stalin was not at all in agreement with the plan for a Balkan federation. He said: "Dimitrov is still behaving as if he were the Secretary-General of the Comintern."[16] Dimitrov quickly abandoned his notion of a Balkan federation and his own ideas on the future development of Bulgaria. At the Fifth Congress of the Bulgarian Communist Party in December 1948, he approved the leading role of the Soviet Union in the Eastern bloc and the validity of its experiences for the other East European countries. He fundamentally altered his theoretical views. Bulgaria's postwar history up to 1948 was divided into two periods, the first from 9 September 1944 to the execution of the peasant leader Nikola Petkov in September 1947, and the second, after September 1947, in which socialist restructuring was begun. In contrast to his declaration of September 1946 that in Bulgaria there would be no dictatorship of the proletariat, Dimitrov stressed explicitly that the People's Republic would combat the vestiges of capitalism in a democratic coalition, with the Soviet Union taking the lead, in the form of a dictatorship of the proletariat. Under his leadership, Bulgaria's social order was wholly adapted to the Soviet model. Soon afterward, in 1949, Georgij Dimitrov died, at the age of 67. His successors have never challenged the principles of the system. Nor have the people ever rebelled against it. Economic growth has been more than satisfactory throughout the entire period. The living standard has risen appreciably.

Even Bulgaria has not been spared the typical disadvantages of a planned economy, however. The declining rationality of the economy induced the party leadership to undertake improvements in the steering model in the mid-'60s.

## THE FIRST REFORM

At the beginning of December 1965, the Politburo guidelines on "A New System for Planning and Management of the Economy" were published.[17] In view of the fact that these guidelines coincided in time with the Soviet economic reform of 1965, it is tempting to view this as a further demonstration of the solidarity of the small Balkan nation with its big brother. Bulgaria also tried Khrushchev's unfortunate experiment with territorial economic administration (*Sownarchosen*). To be sure, Bulgaria is also not immune to the reproach that it has often emulated Soviet solutions, sometimes to the letter. Nevertheless, it would be more just to see Bulgaria's reform of 1965 as an attempt to eliminate the typical defects of a planned economy by means of the typical methods of a planned economy. Bulgaria did not dare to undertake radical changes similar to those undertaken by Czechoslovakia in the Prague Spring or by Hungary at the beginning of 1968, but a number of original solutions may nonetheless be found in Bulgaria's 1965 reform, though it might be somewhat exaggerated to call this a "New System for Planning and Management."

Economic development in the first half of the '60s gave no cause for uneasiness. A decline in economic growth from 9.6 percent yearly in the period from 1955 to 1959 to 7.8 percent in the next five years and a decline in gross output of industry from 14 percent to 11 percent during the same period was still no cause for concern about the future of the country. The cumbersome planning practices and the bureaucratic excesses in administration and the disproportions in the development of a few sectors of the economy and the excess burden placed on the economic reserves were, however, reason enough to improve the steering of the economy.

None of the ingredients of the 1965 measures indicated that fundamental reform of the system was in the offing. Nor did the leadership of the country have any intentions of decentralizing the decision-making powers in the economy. The Politburo guidelines published on 4 December 1965 speak of "improved coordination" and "improved steering and management through central planning," but not of a shift of decision-making powers to the microlevel.

A closer look at the Bulgarian reform leads to the conclusion that the GDR served more as a model than the Soviet Union. The basic features of the "New Economic System for Planning and Management in the GDR" are clearly discernible in the guidelines for the "New System for Planning and Management of the People's Economy" of Bulgaria. Two components of the two reform attempts are fundamentally similar: the reorganization of the administration of industry, and the reorganization of the banking system. In both the GDR and Bulgaria, some decision-making powers were transferred to the newly formed industrial associations, without, however, calling central planning and administration into question. The associations were granted considerable powers in the area of investments; but the basic principles of economic development were to continue to be determined by central planning. The state was also to supervise the course of the economy.

The banking system was restructured in Bulgaria just as in the GDR, if somewhat later. These were the only two East European countries to attempt to transform the banking structure from one typical for a planned economy to a system suited for market conditions: the traditional concept of a state bank, which simultaneously excercises all the functions of commercial banks — controls money circulation, settles claims among firms, and grants credit — was replaced by the concept of a central bank as the "bankers' bank," business operations being left in the hands of the commercial banks. Banking transactions were integrated into the administrative system of the economy as a whole through appropriate refinancing procedures and a differentiated interest-rate schedule.

Pursuant to the government decree of 14 March 1969,[18] which took effect as of 1 April 1969, Bulgaria's national bank was relieved of the functions of a commercial bank. These functions were transferred to two newly established banks, the Bulgarian Industrial Bank and the Bulgarian Agriculture and Trade Bank.

Not only the reasons for the introduced reforms but also the reasons for dismantling the decision-making powers that had been granted to the microlevel at the end of the '60s and beginning of the '70s were the same in both countries. When the inevitable stage was reached at which the decision had to be made either to continue the reforms toward a further decentralization of decision-making, with the corresponding effects this would have on the monopoly position of the ruling party, or to return to the traditional channels of a centrally administered economy, both Bulgaria and the GDR chose the second alternative.

The Bulgarian economic reform of 1965 comprised further changes in the methods of planning and administration, but these differed more quantitatively than qualitatively from the measures undertaken at the same time in the other East European countries. The number of binding indicators of the central plan was reduced to four, namely, the quantity of principal products, the limit for investments, the input of raw materials and fuels, and the volume of foreign-trade turnover. Profitability, defined as the ratio of profit to assets, was to serve as a criterion of efficiency. An end was to be brought to the unfortunate practice of resting the development of enterprise activities mainly on investment projects financed by the state. Enterprises were thenceforth to finance themselves, and a "fund for development and improvement," created from a part of the profits, was to serve as the main source. The lacking funds could be raised through interest-bearing credits from the state bank. To induce the enterprises to make sparing use of their capital and working capital, they were to transfer 6 percent of the value of their working capital to the state budget annually, just as in the other East European countries.

An important component of the measures undertaken to improve planning and administrative practices was the new price system. Three price categories were stipulated: (a) fixed prices for investment and the principal consumer goods; (b) maximum and minimum prices for goods exchanged in trade among enterprises; and (c) free market prices for seasonal products and products from the handicrafts industries.

The measures undertaken in 1965 did not entail a radical reform of the economic system. Although enterprises were given a freer hand in operating, there was no self-administration to speak of. The ministries for the particular sectors of the economy retained their powers as command and supervisory bodies, and the central planning authorities continued to decide the direction of economic development. The technical and organizational improvements made planning practice simpler and more bearable and somewhat reduced bureaucratism in administration. Even these modest reforms, however, soon seemed too radical to the party leaders, especially since they had aroused hopes among management that the introduced liberalization of production relations might mean the first step toward authentic self-administration of the enterprises. The party leaders feared that any further step in the direction of a decentralization of economic powers could lead to the central apparatus's losing its powers. Toward the end of the '60s, therefore, a gradual dismantling of the reform experiment was begun. There can be no doubt that developments in Czechoslovakia in 1968 were decisive for the retreat begun a year later in Bulgaria.

## THE 1965 REFORM WAS IN EFFECT ONLY FOUR YEARS

Bulgaria began somewhat later than the other East European countries with its reform of steering methods, but its experiences were similar. The restructured planning and administrative practices lost their effectiveness over time. For the economic management the reforms did not seem radical enough, but for the party leadership they seemed too dangerous. Even a slight liberalization of the decision-making powers sets uncontrollable economic processes into motion and requires more investment funds than the central authorities find appropriate. Preferential projects become jeopardized. When this happens, a planned economy that is even no more than slightly decentralized loses one of its most important qualities: it ceases to be an economy with politically determined priorities; the party leadership loses control over the economic process as a whole. It should be borne in mind that no matter how much the party leaders may wish to promote initiative at the micro-level, they will never do so at the expense of limiting the monopoly power of the state. Hungary is still trying to find a middle way, and the other East European countries have opted for the omnipotence of the central plan. If the time between the easing and the retightening of the reins was somewhat shorter in Bulgaria than elsewhere, external rather than internal factors were chiefly responsible.

There is no talk in Bulgaria of a retreat, since such a term is not in use in the official vocabulary. The talk is of "incongruities" and of overhasty resort to administrative methods that had not been sufficiently tested. At a meeting of the Central Committee in July 1968 the party chief Todor Zhivkov said: "As soon as we had developed the new system, it became clear to us that the proposed mechanism did not fully correspond to the principles and requirements of this system."[19] The steering system, said Zhivkov, "can give the desired results if a suitable way to employ that system can be found." This, according to the party chief, is to be found only "by way of experimentation, through practical testing in the course of using the new system."[20] Zhivkov also spoke of disproportions that had first to be eliminated, and of material, financial, and foreign exchange reserves that were needed to get an effective economic reform under way.

The keynote of this speech, in which he alluded to a return to centralization, was formulated by Bulgaria's party chief as follows: "The building of a socialist society under the conditions of the scientific and technical revolution requires that the proportions in the economy and the structures of the economy be set centrally by the state plan, in accordance with the goals and tasks of the Party's policy for a given period." Though Todor Zhivkov tried to tone down the severity of this statement somewhat — "This does not mean that we are going to revert once again to moderate centralism in planning" — there can be no doubt that the party leaders were no longer keen to undertake any radical reforms. The "Decree No. 50 of the Council of Ministers on the Step-by-Step Application and Further Development of the New System of Management of the Nation's Economy" of 6 November 1968 contemplated further improvements, but decision-making powers were to be centralized rather than decentralized. This trend was evident primarily in the increase in the number of binding plan indicators. The most important contractual deliveries were to be defined in quantity terms. Not only was the scope of investment projects to be centrally determined but the utilization of machinery and equipment would be calculated in quantitative terms in the plan targets. In addition, the expenditure of raw materials and other materials, foreign exchange proceeds and expenditures, and the size of the wages fund were to be determined in the plan, and the indicators for the distribution of profits, differentiated by sector, were to be set centrally.

Economic administration was reorganized to further centralize decision-making powers. Of special importance was the creation of "a committee for economic coordination" for the task of coordinating the activities of ministries and supervising the fulfillment of plan targets. At the same time, economic ministries were enjoined to stay away from the day-by-day management of enterprise activities and to concentrate, in the future, on the longer-term aspects of development and on technical progress. The reorganization of the industrial associations also indicates that the trend was more toward centralization than decentralization. The number of industrial associations was reduced from 120 to 65, and the enterprise associations lost their independence as of 31 December 1970. Soon afterward, the traditional structure typical of a planned economy was restored to the banking system. The national bank, which was to operate as a "bankers' bank," grant no credits, and engage in no clearing activities, resumed the activities of a commercial bank on the basis of a government decree of 12 December 1970. The Investment Bank and the Agriculture and Trade Bank, both just founded in 1969, were merged with the national bank.

## THE TIMES OF INFLATED GROWTH ARE PAST

When Bulgaria took measures in the mid-'60s to relieve the planning and administrative practices of bureaucratic distortions, the growth rates were still at above-average level. The intention was not to accelerate growth, but to structure the economy more symmetrically, put an end to uneconomic expenditure of labor and capital, and give enterprise managements a freer hand for exercising initiative. As has already been noted, the political leaders of the country were never inclined to go so far with decentralization that the state's monopoly on power would be placed into jeopardy, and events in Czechoslovakia reinforced them in their view that liberalization ought either to be fundamental or not take place at all.

If after almost a decade, at the end of the '70s, the reform ideas experienced a renaissance, one reason was because economic growth again began to decline. It was indeed clear that the economy could not develop so rapidly in the second industrialization phase as in the *Sturm und Drang* period, but the decline came at a time when the needs of the population were still far from satisfied. Although Bulgaria can nonetheless be proud of its economic growth, its standard of living is lower than in similarly developed market economies.

The results not only are still under the plan targets but have even declined perceptibly. In 1980 the national income was 3 percentage points lower, and the gross industrial output was even 6.8 percentage points lower, than the yearly average in the five-year period from 1965 to 1970. Retail trade turnover was also much lower. Foreign trade increased at an above-average rate, in 1982 by 9.1 percent, reaching 21,600 million leva. The growth rate of the national income has decreased from year to year: from 7 percent in

1976 to 6.3 percent in 1977, 6 percent in 1978, and 4 percent in 1981. The planned economic growth for the five-year period 1976–1980 (48 percent) was only 40 percent achieved. Industrial production rose by 35 percent instead of the planned 55 percent. Machine construction grew at an above-average rate by 56.2 percent, and the chemistry industry grew by 52.9 percent, but the metallurgical industry by only 18.1 percent. Gross agricultural output remained far below plan targets: for the entire five-year period it increased by only 12 percent instead of 22 percent; the total agricultural production in 1982 exceeded 8,660 million leva.

Indicators of Economic Growth in Bulgaria
(Average Annual Changes, in Percent)

| | 1965–1970 | 1971–1975 | 1976–1980 | 1980 | Plan 1981–1985 |
|---|---|---|---|---|---|
| Produced national income | 8.7 | 7.5 | 6.1 | 5.7 | 4.6–5.4 |
| Gross industrial output | 10.9 | 9.1 | 6.2 | 4.1 | 5.4–6.2 |
| Gross agricultural output | 3.5 | 3.0 | 0.8 | –4.9 | 6.1–6.6 |
| Labor productivity in industry | 6.9 | 6.8 | 6.1 | 2.6 | 6.3–6.6 |
| Gross capital investment | 12.5 | 8.6 | 4.5 | 12.7 | 3.7 |
| Retail trade turnover | 8.7 | 7.7 | 4.3 | 5.4 | 3.7–4.0 |
| Average wages and salaries | 6.1 | 3.3 | 4.4 | 9.7 | 2.7 |
| Exports | 11.3 | 14.1 | 14.5 | 16.3 | 7.0 |
| Imports | 9.2 | 19.6 | 9.5 | 11.7 | 7.0 |

Sources: Statistical yearbooks, as well as Planerfüllungsbericht sowie Wochenbericht, des Deutschen Institutes für Wirtschaftsforschung, 25/81.

Agriculture suffers from structural problems and an acute shortage of labor. By the end of 1968, 3,290 cooperatives had merged to form 857 large collectives, and 205 state farm enterprises had merged to form 19 large enterprises. After the Central Committee Plenary Session of April 1970, agro-industrial complexes of a magnitude of 30,000 hectares and 50,000 people were formed by merging cooperatives and agrarian and industrial state enterprises. Social policy as well as purely economic reasons played a role in the decision to form these complexes. The intent was to alter the settlement structure, i.e., to form agrocities instead of village agglomerations. Importance was also attached to retaining property relations and democratic leadership.

These goals were not achieved. Since the mid-'70s there has been a trend toward a restoration of autonomy to the cooperatives and the state agricultural enterprises. In only 24 of the total of 143 agro-industrial complexes have the members preserved their identity.[21] The chief drawback was that these huge complexes could not be equipped with adequate industrial technology; the managerial functions were excessively centralized, and the decision-making powers of the micro-units were reduced to a minimum. Collective leadership lost its significance as a basic principle in the agricultural cooperatives. Although in 1978 a few measures were also undertaken to eliminate these shortcomings, the organizational framework seemed too huge and unwieldy for the available technology to cope with. The hope that rural living conditions would be brought up to approximately the level of urban conditions through the formation of these agro-industrial complexes has not been realized, and the flight from the countryside has increased.

While the decline in the number of people employed in agriculture from 3,325,000 in 1948 to 2,262,000 in 1960 was attributable to efforts to reduce the overpopulation in the countryside and to rapid urbanization as a result of accelerated industrialization, and indeed was regarded as a positive aspect of the restructuring of Bulgaria into an industrial state, neither the rural areas nor the cities were later prepared for any further migration – agriculture because of inadequate mechanization, and the cities because of a shortage of housing. In 1975 the number of people employed in agriculture decreased to 2,224,000,[22] and then by 20,000 a year in subsequent years. Those who migrated were mostly young people; as a result, the average age of agricultural workers has increased considerably. The party leaders undertook some far-reaching measures to stop the flight from the countryside: people with specialized skills who participate directly in production receive a 30–40 percent higher wage than those who perform administrative functions; livestock breeders receive a bonus for uninterrupted service on a farm; a pension insurance was introduced, and other social services were improved considerably. But the lack of specialists is acute: the number of skilled farm workers decreased from 100,000 in 1975 to 75,000 in 1979. Bulgarian agriculture clearly has too few reserves to increase its efficiency.

## BULGARIA'S FOREIGN TRADE IS ORIENTED TOWARD THE EAST, BUT THE COUNTRY IS INDEBTED TO THE WEST

The socialist countries accounted for 70.5 percent of Bulgaria's exports and 79 percent of imports in 1980,[23] whereas the corresponding figures for the OECD are 20.3 percent and 17 percent, respectively. Nonetheless, Bulgaria is indebted to the West. The gross debt reached $4,180 million at the end of 1979, and net debt reached $3,640 million.[24]

More than three years of exports at the 1980 export volume would be necessary to eliminate the accrued debt. The debt is considerable if one takes into account that 38 percent of 1979 exports were used to cover the debt service. The interest rates are especially oppressive. In the period from 1976 to 1979, $1,260 million in interest was paid, including $373 million in 1978 and $470 million in 1979.[25]

However, the foreign trade deficit to the West is still growing, as the following figures show.

| | 1977 | 1978 | 1979 | 1980 |
|---|---|---|---|---|
| | | (in Millions of Dollars) | | |
| Exports | 398.6 | 481.5 | 707.7 | 795.6 |
| Imports | 830.7 | 1,017.2 | 1,136.0 | 1,561.1 |
| Foreign trade deficit | 432.1 | 535.7 | 428.3 | 765.5 |

Source: U.S. Department of Commerce, U.S.-Bulgarian Trade Terms, I–XII 1980. Washington, D.C., April 1981.

Although Bulgaria was able to transform its trade deficit ($74 million in 1975) with the CMEA countries into a surplus of $81 million in 1980, the deficit in foreign trade with the West has remained considerable. After a decline from $535.7 billion in 1978 to $428.3 million in 1979, the foreign trade deficit in 1980 rose to $765.5 million. Imports increased by 37.4 percent and exports by only 12.4 percent. With a share of 31.9 percent in imports and 24.4 percent in exports (1980), the Federal Republic of Germany is the most important trading partner of Bulgaria in the West, followed by France (share in imports, 10.9 percent; in exports, 24.4 percent) and Italy (10.9 percent and 36.6 percent, respectively).[26] Austria is one of Bulgaria's most important Western trade partners outside the Common Market: in 1980 it had a 6.6 percent share in Bulgaria's exports and a 7.8 percent share in her imports. Bulgaria's debt to Austria (921 million shillings at the end of 1980) is equivalent to 155 percent of the annual exports (1980: 594 million shillings). In 1981 and 1982 Bulgaria was capable of reducing the trade deficit and stabilizing the indebtedness at the 1980 level.

## MUCH LOWER GROWTH RATES

Bulgaria has no more factors for dynamic economic growth. The plan targets have become more modest, as may be seen from the following figures:

| | 1976–1980 | | 1981-1985 |
|---|---|---|---|
| | Growth, in percent | | |
| | Plan | Actual | Plan |
| National income | 48–52 | 40 | 25–30 |
| Industrial product | 55–60 | 35 | 30–35 |
| Agricultural output | 20 | 12 | 20–22 |
| Income of the population (real) | 20 | 12.7 | 16–18 |

Nevertheless, the traditional development model is stubbornly maintained: stress continues to be laid on forcing heavy industry as the "basic pillar of the economy." It will absorb the greater part of the investments projected for the current five-year period (about $42 billion). The people's incomes will increase by half as much as the national income. The guidelines for the current five-year plan concentrate on rationalization and modernization of the available potential — only 30 percent of the total investments are to be used for new construction — and on accelerating technical progress, saving energy, and increasing individual productivity. Some stimuli are expected from the second reform in planning and steering practices instituted in early 1980.

## THE SECOND REFORM

The lesson learned from the first reform in the mid-'60s is that overall management of the economy has to remain in the hands of the party leadership. The technical and organizational measures taken in early 1980 were nevertheless more comprehensive and more substantial than those of the first reform. All possible means within the existing system were used to rationalize planning. The organization structure was improved, and combines were created along with the industrial associations; some of these are organized horizontally and others, vertically. The decisive reason for their creation was probably that, through concentration of resources, they would make more rapid technical progress possible. The combines not only are to be engaged in a specific production activity but also are responsible for marketing, research, domestic trade, foreign trade, and the completion of investment projects.

The principal aims of the reform in 1980 were to make the enterprises self-supporting and to achieve a complete and socially defensible coverage of costs and exact economic accounting. The central authorities were to retain only those levers of economic control that are essential for maintaining the direction of development and for fulfilling the centrally set goals. Decision-making powers that do not come into conflict with centrally planned projects were delegated to the microlevel. It was explicitly stressed that the central authorities had no right to intervene in the internal affairs of enterprises, to modify their functioning, or to deprive them of direct control over production. The central authorities may not impose their decisions on enterprises; they have material responsibility for their own recommendations.

The number of binding indicators was once again reexamined and reduced by half. The main range of goods has remained binding, and these must not only be produced but also sold. The net product, export proceeds, maximum number of employees, use of important raw materials and other materials, investment in machinery and equipment, and volume of foreign currency necessary for imports are also prescribed centrally.

The principle that prices should be sufficient to cover costs was abandoned, and the world price level was accepted as a guideline. In December 1979, both wholesale and retail prices were raised, and corresponding adjustments were made in the wage schedules.

The purport of the reform initiative made in 1981 was not to abandon the economic units to the free play of market forces. They were bound by a whole edifice of comprehensive rules that were to aid in the attainment of the centrally set goal. The entire set of state norms and standards, which cover the most important material and financial aspects of economic activities, are intended to establish the preconditions for enterprises to become self-supporting within the bounds set by the central authorities.

The advantage of this steering method consists, in the opinion of Bulgarian economist Georgij Krumov,[27] in the fact that it creates an economic constraint in order to increase labor productivity, to bring wages into line with socially defensible costs, and to improve the quality and efficiency of the economy's performance.

In the reformed steering system, the enterprise enters into equivalent commodity and money relations with the other economic units;

it forms and distributes financial funds and acquires values, which it controls itself. The enterprise also enters into relations with the finance and credit system of the state, in that it transfers a certain portion of its income to the state budget and obtains interest-bearing bank credits. The economic unit makes decisions, within the limits defined by universally applicable state norms and centrally set plan targets, and bears full responsibility for these decisions, which must, however, conform to the standard guidelines and procedures for income distribution. First, the prescribed payments to the state budget and monies to replenish the fund of the territorial authorities are paid out, followed by interest on bank loans taken to supplement working capital, insurance fees, and the debt service on investment credits. Then come payments to the branch ministries and industrial associations, and payments to replenish the development fund and the fund for technical progress. These obligations are binding on the enterprise, regardless of its financial yields. Depreciation standards are established centrally. The ministries, the industrial associations, and the territorial authorities each receive 1 percent, and the development fund and the fund for technical progress each 4 percent, of a firm's income. Enterprises can no longer expect subsidies from state budgets. Subsidies are granted only in exceptional cases, when unprofitable products are manufactured within the framework of the approved plan targets. A firm is exempted from fees paid to the state budget only if objective reasons can be demonstrated why it cannot pay even the prescribed minimum fee.

The improved steering methods introduced in the early '80s should be able to contribute, to some degree, to an improvement in efficiency. In general, these new methods are compatible with the existing authoritarian system, which, however, does not appear any longer to fit the social and economic level Bulgaria has now achieved. Bulgaria enters the '80s with a burden of debt that is already 15 percent of the annual national product. Although the five-year plan for 1981 to 1985 takes into account a decline in growth, financing of the modest planned growth will encounter considerable difficulties since the debt has already exceeded tolerable limits. The debt cannot be allowed to grow further; it must be reduced.

The Bulgarians are also well aware that fundamental changes are necessary, but hesitate to embark on them. It is questionable whether the improved paraphrenalia of economic control is in itself sufficient to achieve even the now more modest goals of the current five-year plan.

# 4

# Romania's Independent Path within the Traditional Framework

In analyzing the contradictory development of Romania, one is faced with the enigma of why just this country, which has struggled to gain a remarkable margin of freedom in the two Eastern organizations, the Warsaw Pact and the CMEA, is nonetheless still closer to the Soviet model than the other East European countries, which are less emancipated in terms of foreign policy, but are more disposed to reform. This complicated question cannot be answered unequivocally, but some clues may be gained from an examination of the development of the social system within the specifically Romanian context.

Romania's stubborn struggle for national independence, which has gone on for almost twenty years, derives, in the first place, from the facts that hardly any other nation has had its national sensibilities more severely wounded and that no aspect of resistance can forge solidarity between a people and its leaders better than the struggle for national self-assertion. Romania's sovereignty was threatened just before and after World War II by the Soviet drive for conquest, first as a result of the Ribbentrop-Molotov agreement of 17 August 1939, which permitted the Soviets to annex North Bukovina and Bessarabia, which Russia had once before conquered in 1877, but had returned to Romania through the Versailles Treaty. No other Eastern country had such concrete grounds to feel imperiled. The desire to regain the lost territories was one of the principal reasons that Romania, which fought on the side of the Entente in World War I after 1916, in World War II joined the Axis powers and regained the lost territories in alliance with Hitler's Germany. Although on 23 August 1944, nine months before the end of the war, the king, supported by the Romanian Communists, overthrew the Antonescu government, disavowed the alliance with Hitler's Germany, and declared war on Germany on 25 August 1944, and the Romanian

Army participated in the liberation of Czechoslovakia and Hungary, the Soviet Union did not renounce the territories it had annexed in its pact with Hitler.

It might be mentioned in passing that the Soviet Union, which was already on Romania's borders, received the news of the new government with Communist participation without enthusiasm. It was not disposed to spare Romania the fate of a conquered nation. It would have been easier for the Soviet Union to dictate the terms of peace to a defeated Antonescu than to a government that had declared war on its former allies several months before the end of the war. The Central Committee of the Romanian Communist Party, in November 1961, not unjustly reproached the "Moscovites" (the leading group in the party who had returned from the Soviet Union after the war) for wanting to prevent the participation of the Communists in the royal *coup d'état* of August 1944 and for having preferred that the land be conquered by the Soviet Army.[1] It would also not be incorrect to say that not only the painful shrinkage of national territory but also the fact that a country that had already been converted to communism was still treated as a former enemy and had to pay reparations aroused deep antagonisms, which have hardly diminished in virulence to this very day.

Indeed, the Soviet Union wanted everything: both an obedient regime, i.e., one led by Communists, the territories annexed before the war in the alliance with Hitler, and, over and above all this, huge reparations as well. All was obtained, as the Romanian regime was too weak to resist. In the period between the wars, the illegal Communist Party of Romania numbered no more than 2,000 members.

The path was embarked upon systematically. First, the way to power was paved for the Communists with the aid of the well-tested "salami" tactic. The Soviet Union tolerated the National Democratic Coalition of Social Democrats, Liberals, Caranists (peasants party), and Communists formed in August 1944 for only a short time. On 6 March 1945 the Soviet commander-in-chief in Romania, Andrei Vyshinskii, carried out the final *coup d'état*. A government dominated by the Communists was formed under the leadership of Petru Groza, who sympathized with the Communists. Twenty days later, the economic and political transformations were begun that were to establish a Soviet-type social system in Romania. It should be noted that some of these transformations enjoyed the general approval of the population. This was especially true of the agrarian reform, which had been started as far back as 1918–1921, but had never been completed, and of which the peasants had long dreamed. No one, then, could even have suspected that the land granted to the poorest would later be collectivized, together with the old landowners' property.

Communist influence was strengthened considerably, not only by the agrarian reform but also by the belief, deliberately propagated, that the Communist Party alone was to thank for the fact that the Seven Mountains, ceded to Romania after World War I, but inhabited primarily by Hungarians, had remained Romanian. The democratic bloc, controlled by the Communists, emerged victorious in the elections of 1946 partly because of this influence but also, and principally, because of the Communists' endless manipulations. Thereafter events followed the usual pattern: in 1947 the Caranists, the Liberals, led by G. Tatarescu, and some of the Social Democratic Party were forced to step down from the government. The compliant remains of the once-influential Social Democratic Party was incorporated into the Communist Party of Romania on 23 February 1948. Until just a short time before, Romania had always been a kingdom, and as late as 8 November 1946, the Communists had wished the king a long life in good health. But an abrupt end was being prepared for his reign. On 30 December 1947, the king abdicated, and Romania was declared a People's Republic. In June 1948, another, this time decisive, step was taken toward the Sovietization of Romanian society. A decree was issued nationalizing industry, the banks, and the transport system. Nationalization of the means of production was pursued at a breakneck pace: in 1949, 85 percent, and in 1952, 92 percent, of industrial manufacture was owned by the state. In 1949 collectivization of agriculture was begun. By the beginning of the '50s, Romania was transacting half of its foreign trade with the Soviet Union, with which it had had only negligible economic relations in the period between the wars.

Sovietization, introduced under the leadership of the Romanian Communist Party and the Soviet advisers, did not save the country from reparation payments. Nor were these slight, considering the level of development of the country at the time: the $300 million (on the basis of the 1938 exchange rate and prices) Romania had to pay to the Soviet Union accounted for 37.5 percent of the state budget of 1946 and 1947 and 46.6 percent of the budget for the next year.[2] The cash Romania had to pay was, however, only a fraction of the total reparations bill. As in the case of East Germany, the greatest burden was the Soviet Romanian enterprises, the *Sovroms*, formed just after the war. Sixteen "joint" companies were formed in the most important economic sectors of the country, especially in the oil industry and in sea and air transportation. What was most interesting, however, was how the "joint" founding capital was raised. Whereas Romania had to invest effective values, the Soviet Union's contribution (50 percent of the total capital) was in the form of German property in Romania that had been expropriated. Yet when the "joint" enterprises were dissolved after Stalin's death, Romania had to pay back the larger part of the Soviet share in "hard" goods.[3]

## THE PATH TO NATIONAL COMMUNISM

Obviously, the occupation practices, though camouflaged with slogans of liberation, did not leave the people with fond memories, and the governing party that had to defend this hostile policy of the "Big Brother" hardly acquired a good reputation. The belief, nurtured by a considerable segment of the people, that the new social system would serve the welfare faded. In the new state system, which presented itself as a kind of "dictatorship of the proletariat," the Romanian workers continued to lead the lives of wage laborers, as in the time of Ion Antonescu. A powerful elite formed — a new hierarchical ruling bureaucracy that adopted the life-style of capitalism, but not its zeal and creative spirit. The Communist Party grew steadily in numbers, while its ideological impact declined proportionately. It had no experience in governing a state, and blindly followed the instructions of its Soviet advisers, even in the struggle against real and supposed enemies of the state. The experienced and highly educated elite of the _ancien régime_ was quickly eliminated. A bitter power struggle flared up among the Party leadership itself, and the most intelligent and most enterprising minds became its victims. Lucretiu Patrascanu, the coalition partner of the royal government that overthrew Ion Antonescu in August 1944, suffered the same sad fate. He was executed in April 1953, to be rehabilitated 20 years later. In May 1952, a group of leading Communists, including Ana Pauker, Teohari Georgescu, and Vasile Luca, were expelled from the Party.[4]

Industrialization, pursued with overambitious investment projects, invariably at the cost of agriculture, consumption, and housing, has left some sad memories behind it. The hope that sooner or later it would produce an abundance of consumer goods rapidly faded. The gap between broad strata of the population and the ruling elite deepened. The need to create an ideology that would gloss over the worn slogans of "real socialism," by then discredited, became ever more urgent. There was no mass uprising in Romania as in East Germany in 1953, in Hungary and Poland in 1956. The working class was too young and inexperienced. The intelligentsia, decimated in the initial postwar period, mounted no resistance to speak of. Gheorghe Gheorgiu-Dej, who had maintained an autocratic rule since 1952 when the Pauker-Luca group was expelled, was no dreamer who aspired to replacing real socialism with a socialism with a human face. And there was no Dubček to be found among the aspirers to the post of First Party Secretary who would have been willing to introduce far-reaching economic and political reforms. Under these conditions only one ideology seemed capable of motivating the people, the ideology of Romanian nationalism. But stress on national self-sufficiency and independence and a link with the proud traditions of Romanians as the descendants of the Romanized Dakers were not sufficient. These traditions were much too remote; and the Communist Party, worn out and tired, its reserve of talent dried up, was still seen as a representative of foreign interests and an alien body. The present, marked by Soviet domination, was more important than historical reminiscences and memories of a glorious past. Much courage was necessary to combat it. Gheorghiu-Dej had been able to make the transition from the Stalinist period to the post-Stalin period without any special difficulties or notable reforms. Now it was he as well who embarked upon this risky path. He skillfully exploited the controversies within the Soviet leadership and the external difficulties of the Soviet Union to create for himself as broad a margin of freedom as possible within the given geopolitical conditions. After the serious clash beteen Khrushchev and the Molotov group in 1957, which made the Soviet leadership poorer by four old Stalinists, Romania was able, one year later, to secure the withdrawal of Soviet troops.

A further step forward in the same direction was made after Khrushchev initiated the second de-Stalinization phase at the Twenty-second Party Congress of the CPSU. At the Congress of the Central Committee of the Communist Party of Romania in November and December 1961, the party leader proudly declared that he had carried out de-Stalinization at the very peak of Stalinism. The Moscovite group, expelled in 1952 and now forgotten, was once again invoked as part of a public condemnation of the traditions of obeisance to Moscow. But the day of reckoning with the grim past did not occur until after the Soviet–Chinese conflict had significantly undermined the status of the Soviet Union in the Communist world. At that time, Romania felt its economic interests threatened by Khrushchev's proposal to revive the CMEA, which at that time had been pronounced dead. For Khrushchev, economic integration was the best means of cementing solidarity among the East European countries, weakened by the Hungarian uprising and the split over China. Spurred by Gomulka, who had made a comeback in October 1956 and regarded Eastern integration, shored up by liberal forces of the country, as the only means of eliminating as quickly as possible, those "revisionist" elements foreign to him, Khrushchev presented his plan to steer the East European countries with a joint economic plan, introduce international cooperative and joint ventures, and make economic integration the most important instrument of political community.

Khrushchev's intention of binding the Eastern bloc countries more closely to the Soviet Union with the aid of economic integration triggered protests from the Romanian leadership. At the CMEA Congress in March 1963, Gheorgiu-Dej declared that his country was determined to fight against transforming the CMEA into an international economic executive organ and against the plan to "cement" the existing structure of the division of labor, which confined Romania to the role of supplier of agricultural products. The Romanian party leadership saw this plan as a major danger for industrialization, which had already been initiated, especially for heavy industry, whose products were to be sold in East European markets, while advanced know-how was to be procured from the West. The party leader reminded his partners that one of the principal tasks of the CMEA was to raise the economies of the less-developed countries to the level of the more highly developed ones. Romania has never, even to this day, been able to count on any noteworthy economic aid from the CMEA countries. The developed industrial countries in Eastern Europe, the GDR and Czechoslovakia, then as now oppose a radical restructuring of the division of labor within the CMEA. To continue the industrialization of the country, Romania was forced to have recourse to the aid of Western banks and, since 1972, the Bretton Woods institutions as well.

The hard debate within the CMEA was, of course, not the only cause of the eruption of the long-simmering crisis in Romanian–

Soviet relations; but it was the igniting spark. On 26 April 1964, the time had come. The Communist Party of Romania declared before the world at large that it was not willing to submit to the orders of another party. The declaration stated:

> It is the exclusive right of every party to set its own political line, its concrete objectives, and the ways and means to achieve those objectives independently.... The relation of class forces in a particular country, the shifts in power, the fluctuating mood of the masses, and the special internal and external conditions of a country are known by no one more precisely and thoroughly than the Communist Party of the country concerned.[5]

Eleven months later, Gheorgiu-Dej died suddenly, at the age of 62. His successor, Nicolae Ceaușescu, made no secret of the fact that he intended to continue along the path of national independence the dead leader had begun. Not only declarations but tangible deeds followed. To name only a few: the unconditional resumption of diplomatic relations with Bonn on 31 January 1967, which at the time was viewed as a violation of alliance loyalty; the refusal of the Prime Minister, J. Maurer, to affix his signature to the Near East Declaration of the Eastern Countries on 9 June 1967; the maintenance of diplomatic relations with Israel; total rejection of any dictate from without. On 24 July 1967, Ceaușescu declared before the great National Assembly that "World problems are no longer the exclusive concern of the great powers." Romania's decision not to participate in the invasion of Czechoslovakia by the five Eastern countries was stalwart and brave, and Ceaușescu's declaration of 21 August 1968 was couched in extremely tough terms: "It is inconceivable that a socialist country, or that socialist countries, should trample the freedom and independence of another state under foot... the Romanian people as a whole will never permit anyone to violate the territory of our fatherland."[6]

In December 1972, Romania joined the International Monetary Fund (IMF) and the World Bank. Romania had never joined the chorus of massive criticism directed by Eastern Europe against China and had always maintained a balanced policy in relation to Moscow and Peking. The Romanian government has conducted a thoroughly independent policy in the Third World and let it be known in unequivocal terms that it disapproved of the intervention in Afghanistan. The country's attitude toward Poland is also unequivocal. Without going so far as to support the reform movement, the Romanian politicians have repeatedly stressed that surmounting the Polish crisis was exclusively the affair of the Polish people.

## BUT NO COMPREHENSIVE REFORMS

Considerable courage was necessary to assert national independence in the existing geopolitical circumstances. No other member of the Warsaw Pact had until then dared to do so with such resoluteness and consistency. With this struggle Romania's leadership made an unmistakable contribution to placing international relations on a more equitable basis. Though it had been willing and able to free the country from Soviet tutelage in regard to foreign relations, it neither could nor would eliminate the fundamental principle of a one-party regime and state-controlled economy; for over the course of time, in Romania as in the other East European countries, social and power structures have emerged that the ruling elite could not sacrifice without acting counter to their own vitally important interests.

And though there can be no doubt that bureaucratic absolutism and a centrally administered economy have come into acute contradiction with the developed production capacities, the ruling elite is still not willing to decentralize, i.e., to liberalize, economic control. It is quite aware that a consistent decentralization of economic control is incompatible with a dirigist state structure. The ruling elite of the country is not willing to forgo its privileged status within the society. Only pressure from below might be able to move the leadership to reforms. At present, however, there is no oppositional mass movement in Romania that could assume a decisive influence on the fate of the country.

## MODIFICATIONS IN THE CENTRALLY ADMINISTERED SYSTEM

Like the leaders of Czechoslovakia and Hungary, who in 1967 were on the threshold of fundamental economic reforms, Romania's party leaders acknowledged that comprehensive planning and centrally administered control were not an adequate steering system for an industrially developed economy. Indeed, the growth rates were still above average at that time, and it was not economic growth that was considered in danger, but efficiency, which was low enough to be cause for serious concern. The input of labor and capital was too high. But although it had been realized that a centrally administered economy had to rely mainly on extensive factors, and that the resources it wasted were becoming increasingly scarce, the Romanian party leadership understood that an economic reform would inevitably have political consequences that would jeopardize the absolute authority of the central apparatus.

The Romanian party leaders therefore did not want reform in the real sense of the term. They did not want to modify the existing steering system, but rather to undertake certain changes in it. The decree entitled "On Measures to Ameliorate Steering and Planning and to Improve the Territorial Administrative Organization," adopted at the National Party Conference in December 1967, documents that technical and organizational measures, not fundamental economic reforms, were intended. Ceaușescu spoke of "improving and adapting" the excessive centralism; J. Maurer, Prime Minister at the time, stressed: "It would be absolutely inconceivable for socialism to develop without planning, without concentration, and without uniform steering"; and his deputy, Niculescu-Mizil, said, "We will not leave the solution of our problems to the blind forces of the free market."[7] In an improved and refined steering system, the party and the central state authorities should, it was said, by no means leave the reins of economic control hang loosely; if anything, they should be drawn tauter. The economy should be administered elastically, to be sure; but the role of the state and the party should even "grow and reach a qualitatively higher level," said Ceaușescu.[8] Two years later, he lent emphasis to this view when he merged the post of party chief with that of head of state, in December 1969.

The technical and organizational measures undertaken in a series of steps over the next two years to shape planning and administration more elastically differed negligibly from those that were being applied at that time in the other Eastern countries: economic administration was restructured; the industrial enterprises were no longer to be subordinated to the newly formed industrial associations. Ten such associations were established, as an experiment, in the fourth quarter of 1967. In the autumn of 1969, the restructuring was complete: 197 industrial associations accounted for the most important sectors of the country's economy.

An important decision was made to eliminate the isolation of the industrial enterprises from foreign markets. While fundamentally maintaining the monopoly over foreign trade, in early 1970 a large number of foreign trade enterprises (12 of a total of 20) were placed directly under the industrial associations. These enterprises were empowered to carry out transactions with their foreign partners and to assume financial responsibility for these transactions. The rules of the classic foreign trade monopoly were altered: whereas traditionally exported and imported goods were cleared in domestic prices with both manufacturer and consumer, thenceforth prices were set more closely to the world market prices. The executive powers of the Ministry of Foreign Trade for safeguarding the interests of the state monopoly were much more strongly emphasized, than in the Hungarian reform of 1968, for instance. The conclusion of foreign trade agreements, the allocation of hard currency, the issuing of import-export licenses, and the basic management of foreign trade were functions that remained in the hands of the ministry.

Planning practices were simplified, and the number of binding indicators was reduced. Seven were to be criteria for evaluating firm activity: sold and paid-for output, the wages fund, maximal expenditure per 1,000 lei of input, labor productivity, maximal investment expenditure, deliveries to the domestic market, and export quotas.[9] The state plan was to be more comprehensive than before the reform. It was to contain indicators for both state and cooperative enterprises. The directives of October 1967 state: "Any tendency to exclude any branch of the economy from planning is injurious, may cause imbalances, and introduces anarchistic market elements into production, sales, and distribution."[10]

The measures undertaken in 1967 to perfect planning and administration of the economy brought about no essential changes in the principles of the Romanian steering system. The nation's economy continued to be steered by a central plan and state administration. And, as had occurred so often before in the history of Eastern Europe, the steering system, with its new minor reforms, gradually returned to the traditional channels of a centrally administered economy. Planning became more comprehensive, and state controls, more stringent. Though many variations of market and planned economies no doubt exist, their basic principles are determined by the form of property and the political system. The shortcomings that are thought finally to have been surmounted by state intervention or by loosening the reins of the state reemerge, slowly but surely. And this is what happened in Romania at the end of the '60s. At the Plenary Session of the Central Committee in December 1969, i.e., three years after the Central Committee decision to perfect the steering methods, Ceaușescu said:

> Often plan indicators are not drawn up on the basis of a thorough study of the facts or the actual potential of enterprises, but rather on the basis of general presumptions.... These practices must cease, because they make planning a mere instrument for justifying and tolerating deplorable affairs rather than an instrument for rational control of the economy.[11]

The practices criticized by the party leader have never ceased. In the early '70s, the measures undertaken in 1967 had already fallen into oblivion.

The productive forces continued to conflict with the antiquated production relations. Toward the end of the '70s, Romania's economy entered into a crisis of control typical of the planned economies, with drastic supply problems, a growing gap between labor-, material- and energy-intensive production capacities and shrinking resources, and chronic balance-of-payments deficits.

## ROMANIA'S ECONOMIC DIFFICULTIES

The conclusion of an analysis recently undertaken by the Wharton Econometric Forecasting Association states "Romania is an excellent candidate for becoming the next Poland in Eastern Europe." At first glance this assessment seems to contradict the considerable growth rates within the country. Although economic growth has indeed fallen off in the last two years, it is still above average by Western standards. Moreover, an economic recession in the Western sense, with high unemployment and high inflation, is today hardly a characteristic of crisis typical of the planned economies alone. Poland is a case in point: just before the deepest crisis in its postwar history, the growth rates in Poland were average or above average.

Nor has Romania been spared the symptoms of crisis characteristic of a planned economy. Industrialization, with priority continually given to heavy industry at the expense of agriculture and the production of consumer goods, carried out with an inflated investment rate, has severely strained the country's means without having thereby achieved the envisaged objective: in Europe, only Turkey and Albania have a lower per capita national income than Romania.[12] Continuation of plans for industrialization,with an investment rate at a level comparable with the earlier one, has become impossible because of the crisis in supply and the growing debt.

Gigantic energy-intensive and material-intensive capacities were constructed that came increasingly to depend upon imports. An unbridgeable gap grew between the rapidly rising need for imports and available export capacities. The country gradually approached the bearable limits of credit.

What was once the kingpin of the country's economy, the oil industry, is no longer capable of keeping pace with the vastly expanded economic potential of the country: in the last five-year period, production has decreased by one-fifth, but consumption has increased by one-third. As late as 1976, oil and oil derivatives were still able to chalk up an active balance ($18 million) in foreign trade, but by 1980 there was a deficit of $2 billion. All the evidence indicates that the extremely rigorous centralized steering system of Romania has become inefficient. There is no evidence, however, that it is amenable to reform. The economic reforms initiated in 1972 were of no lasting consequence. Even the components of the technical know-how imported from the West were incapable, given Romania's ossified steering system, of achieving the desired breakthrough. Currently an attempt is being made to break away from the dirigist steering system, with its fear of innovation, and to introduce new measures. But the political regime in Romania is more autocratic and monopolistic than anywhere else in Eastern Europe. Major decentralization of decision-making powers, which is an indispensable condition for more creative and efficient economic functioning, is scarcely compatible with a state system of this type.

## SHRINKING AND DISPROPORTIONATE ECONOMIC GROWTH

The annual average growth rate (7.1 percent) in the five-year period from 1976 to 1980 was 3.2 percentage points higher than the CMEA average. But this growth rate must be measured by Romanian standards. The aims are high because there is much more ground than average to be made up. Above all, however, the disproportions and gaps in supply are considerable, and efforts to surmount them rely heavily on an inflated growth rate. Thus, the results actually achieved must be compared with those of the preceding period and with the plan targets. The comparison shows that the growth rates in the second half of the '70s (7.1 percent) were lower than in the first half of the decade (11.3 percent) and also lower than those targeted in the plan (10–11 percent). The gradual decline in the growth rate over this five-year period is noteworthy: from 10.5 percent in 1976, to 9.0 percent, 7.4 percent, and 6.2 percent in the next three years, respectively, and 2.5 percent in 1980.

Romania's economic development shows signs of crisis typical of the Eastern countries, not only because of the decline in the growth rates but also because of the unbearable strain of a growth model oriented toward heavy industry. Agriculture is no longer capable of bearing the main burden of industrialization or of fulfilling the tasks of primitive accumulation imposed upon it. The collectivized agricultural complexes, which do not have sufficient machinery and fertilizer, are relatively unproductive and extremely sensitive to fluctuations in the weather; the discrepancy between the city and the countryside in terms of quality of life, which is almost unbridgeable, has meant a steady flight from the countryside, which cannot be compensated for because of insufficient mechanization.

Romania's industry has the typical characteristics of a planned economy. The bureaucracy's inherent tendency toward gigantomania and autarky and the drive to overcome the secular backwardness of the country in the shortest historical time possible have reduced the consumer goods industry to a residual quantity. Its share in total output was no more than 26.3 percent in 1979, while the share of manufacture of the means of production was 73.3 percent, including 34.0 percent for machinery.[13] The untenability of this model has indeed been recognized, but the immeasurable damage that it has caused can hardly be repaired. Ceaușescu himself, who has controlled Romania's destiny for 17 years, had the following to say before the 11,000 delegates to the Second Congress of Agriculture and the Foodstuffs Industry on 19 February 1981: "The primacy of heavy industry at the expense of an intensification and mechanization of agriculture has led to neglect and undersupply of the population and has caused enormous damage to the construction of socialism and communism."

The effect of this growth model, the error of which has been acknowledged much too late, may also be seen in the indicators of economic growth in recent years. In the five-year period from 1976 to 1980, industry expanded at an average growth rate of 9.5 percent (plan target, 10.7 percent) compared with 12.9 percent in the preceding five-year period; the machine-tool industry increased in the last 3 years by 14.3 percent, 11.4 percent, and 10 percent, respectively; the manufacture of construction materials, by 16.2 percent, 12.7 percent, and 5.4 percent, respectively; but the foodstuffs industry, which has suffered from a chronic backlog demand, by only 0.4 percent, 7.9 percent, and 1.1 percent, respectively.[14]

## THE UNFAVORABLE STRUCTURE OF INDUSTRY

The Romanian economy, which has been steered by directives from the central plan authorities, but has never had adequate growth criteria, has been burdened by a distorted price system shielded from the world market, an economically unfounded exchange rate for its currency, and a multilevel industrial infrastructure oriented toward self-sufficiency, and has never been able to develop a correctly proportioned structure among its various branches. This, of course, does not apply to Romania alone. Heavy industry, which has always been the focal point of the state leadership, is also energy-, material- and import-intensive. This growth model was therefore destined sooner or later to encounter insurmountable difficulties. The price explosion accelerated the inevitable disaster. Two branches of industry, namely, the petroleum and steel industries, illustrate the failed economic policy most clearly. For decades oil production was one of the most important branches of Romania's industry. For some time after World War II it was not only able to cover Romania's domestic needs but also brought in considerable hard currency. After a peak year of 14.7 million tons in 1976, oil output decreased steadily. In 1979 it was 12.3 million tons, and in 1980 it was only 11.6 million tons (plan target, 15 million tons). Domestic production is at present 20 percent lower than internal consumption. In the interim, however, the petrochemical industry was considerably expanded, and refinery capacity was increased to 30 million tons. Some of the processed crude oil was exported to the West. But imports far exceeded the value of exports, and the negative balance placed an increasing strain on the country's balance of payments. Oil imports increased from 5 million tons in 1975 to 16 million tons in 1980, but without the available capacities being fully exploited. The foreign trade balance of this branch moved from a surplus of $18 million in 1976 to a deficit of $2 billion in 1980.

Until recently Romania was the only country in Eastern Europe that was not dependent on oil imports from the Soviet Union. But when imports from Iran stopped, Romania was forced to solicit Soviet oil: in 1979, 0.4 million tons, and in 1980, 1.5 million tons, of crude oil were imported from the Soviet Union. Unlike the other CMEA countries, however, which received their oil for a price that until 1982 was 30–40 percent lower than the world market price, Romania must pay the world market price.

Romania's planned economy not only has miscalculated in its structuring of production capacities but also has been wasteful in expenditures, like the other planned economies. One dollar of gross national product requires 2.4 kg of fuels, whereas in France and West Germany, the corresponding figure is only 1 kg.[15] In light of the growing seriousness of the economic situation, a total restructuring of the energy economy was projected. The share of oil in energy consumption was to be reduced from 40 percent in 1980 to 5 percent in 1990, and the share of hydroelectric power was to increase from 17.6 percent to 24 percent and of nuclear energy, from 0 at present to 18 percent.[16]

Economic strategy in steel manufacture is similarly shielded from the world market. Between 1975 and 1980 it increased by 38 percent; at 580 kg of steel per capita in 1979, Romanian steel ranked among the 8 major steel producers in the world. However, the raw materials base, which had always been insufficient, gradually shrank: iron ore production fell from 3 million tons in 1975 to 2.5 million tons in 1979. During the same period iron ore imports had to be increased from 10.9 million to 15 million tons; imports of foundry coke increased from 2.5 million to 2.9 million tons.[17]

The politically motivated goal of achieving autarky in the steel and machine-tool industry seems to be greater than the fear of becoming increasingly more dependent on energy and ore imports. Even the worldwide steel crisis, which creates extremely favorable import conditions, is unable to divert Romania's planners from their economic strategy, which has been outlined many years in advance. In the five-year period from 1981 to 1985, steel output is to increase from 13.175 million tons to 20.4 million tons, and machine construction is to increase by 10.7–11.7 percent annually. The acute shortage of raw materials and energy resources does not seem to have any notable influence on an economic policy aimed at autarky.

## ROMANIA'S ECONOMIC PRIORITIES ARE REFLECTED IN ITS ONE-SIDED INVESTMENT STRUCTURE

Romania's investment rate[18] is the highest rate in the CMEA; in contrast to the other Eastern countries, it shows a rising trend. In 1980 it was 42.5 percent, compared with 34 percent, 39.5 percent, and 40.0 percent in the years 1965, 1970, and 1975, respectively.[19]; in 1980, the total value of gross investments was 212 billion lei (about $14 billion).

The share of the production branches in the total investments, 84 percent, is above average. Not much is left for the other sectors of the economy, e.g., no more than 10 percent for housing construction, and 3.0–3.5 percent for the education and public health sectors.

Industry receives 51 percent of the total sum (6 percent more than in 1965); 75 percent of this is absorbed by 5 branches of industry: energy and fuels, ferrous metallurgy, machinery construction, and the metal-processing industry. Light industry and the foodstuffs industry account for no more than 4.5 percent and 4.4 percent respectively.

Agriculture is the most disadvantaged. For a country such as Romania, however, in which a third of the population is engaged in agriculture, the share in total investments — 14.4–14.5 percent in 1976 and 1977 and 13.9 percent in each of the next two years — is much too low to overcome the considerable backwardness in mechanization and the use of chemical fertilizers.

Investment activities display the same flaws typical of all planned economies, namely, a growing share of incompleted investment projects in total investments, the scattering of scarce investment resources among too many individual projects, and construction times much longer than projected.

## STAGNATING YIELDS FROM AGRICULTURE

The share of agriculture in the national income (16 percent in 1979)[20] is relatively low compared with the relative number of persons employed in agriculture, namely 35 percent, not because productivity in industry and other sectors of the economy is particularly high, but because it is so low in agriculture.

Ninety-two percent of Romania's agriculture is collectivized or in state ownership. Large complexes predominate; but because of insufficient mechanization, they are forced to employ mainly manual labor. Although the invested resources during the five-year period from 1976 to 1980 were 57.3 percent higher than in the preceding five-year period, it proved impossible to reduce to any notable extent the considerable backwardness of agricultural performance.

There is still today only one tractor per 102 hectares of arable land, whereas the figure in the GDR is but 44 hectares, in Czechoslovakia, 50 hectares, and in Bulgaria, 98 hectares. Romania is also backward in electrification, with 170 kw per hectare compared with 605 kw for the GDR, 381 kw for Czechoslovakia, and even 180 kw for Bulgaria.[21] Romania's agriculture is even more backward in the use of fertilizers (124 kg/hectare), a lower figure being found only in the Soviet Union (86 kg/hectare). This figure is one-third the figure for the GDR (358 kg/hectare) and Czechoslovakia (359 kg/hectare), and much lower even than in Hungary (298 kg/hectare) and Bulgaria (220 kg/hectare).

The above-average number of people employed in agriculture (3,582,000 in 1979) and the relatively high number of specialists trained in agriculture (25,420 with secondary and 19,551 with university education)[22] are not able to make up for the inadequate mechanization and use of chemical fertilizers in agriculture. The difference in quality of life between countryside and the city is much greater than in the other East European countries; the flight from the land is also greater. In the last decade, the drain from the countryside was an average of 4.5 percent compared with 3.2 percent in Bulgaria, 2.2 percent in Hungary, 1.9 percent in Czechoslovakia, and 0.8 percent in the Soviet Union.[23] Between 1970 and 1979, the number of people employed in agriculture decreased by 34.2 percent, but the quantity of farm machinery did not increase proportionally. The migrants into the cities are, for the most part, able-bodied men of working age; the proportion of women in the rural labor force is 70 percent in Romania, which is higher than average.

The lack of farm machinery, insufficient fertilizer, and a low level of electrification have negative effects on the yields of agriculture, which is more sensitive to the weather in Romania than in other countries. Fluctuations in annual yields are greater than average: in 1976 gross output increased by 17.3 percent, but in 1977 it declined by 0.9 percent, for various reasons, including floods. In 1978 and 1979 it increased by 3.4 percent and 5.5 percent, respectively, and in 1980 it decreased by 5 percent.[24] The grain yield increased from 15.0 million tons average per year during the first half of the '70s to 19.5 million tons in the second half, but stagnated in the last three years at a level of 19.6 million tons. The potato yield showed a similar development: with an increase from 3.4 million tons average per year during the first half to 4.4 million tons during the second half of the '70s, fluctuating between 4.5, 4.6, and 4.1 million tons in the last three years.[25] Romania's wheat yield per hectare (28.4 double centners) is higher than that of the Soviet Union (15.9), but lower than that of Bulgaria (39.7), Czechoslovakia (33.6), the GDR (43.8), or Hungary (32.6). The corn yield is also lower (33.9 double centners/hectare) than in Bulgaria (37.7), Czechoslovakia (50.1), the GDR (44.9), or Hungary (54.0).[26]

Animal production has also stagnated or declined, although the total quantity of livestock in 1980 was somewhat higher (6,485,000) than in 1976 (6,351,000), and the number of hogs was 11,542,000 in 1980 compared with 10,193,000 in 1976. Meat production was 1,597,000 tons in 1980 compared with 1,760,000 tons in 1979 and 1,582,000 tons in 1978. Milk production decreased from 5,597,000 tons in 1977 and 5,659,000 tons in 1978 to 5,053,000 tons in 1980.[27]

In view of this extremely precarious situation, the party leader proclaimed an "agricultural revolution": by 1985 agriculture is to be transformed into an industrial sector by further mechanization of farm work, raising wages, improving the supply of fertilizers, and carrying out comprehensive irrigation projects. However, the chronic crisis in agriculture has already become a principal cause of the acute supply problems.

## LOW INCOMES AND SCARCE SUPPLY

Between 1976 and 1980 the annual average per capita real income increased by 5.1 percent; the plan (6.2–7 percent), which to a certain degree was to make up for the acute backlog demand, was not fulfilled, and in the last 2 years of the five-year period, the growth rate decreased to 3.3 percent and 3.2 percent, respectively. The average monthly wage of 2,256 lei in 1980 (about $150.40 at the 1 January 1981 exchange rate of 15 lei = $1.00) is rather low. The difference between the maximum and the minimum wage has increased from 43 percent to 56 percent in the last few years as a consequence of measures taken, but is still rather low if one considers that the Eleventh Party Congress of the Polish United Labor Party set the goal of achieving a 50 percent and 350 percent gap, respectively, between the minimum and the maximum wage and the average wage.

The workweek, which is still 48 hours in Romania, is the longest in Europe. The reduction to 46 hours projected for 1981, to be followed by a further decrease to 44 hours somewhat later, was postponed because of the labor shortage caused by low productivity. The increase in consumer goods prices, planned for 1981, was also postponed.

More emphasis is to be placed on incentives for efficient economic management: successful enterprises are authorized to create a bonus fund amounting to 3 percent of planned and 25 percent of above-plan profits. However, a planned economy is still a seller's market. Quality of life depends not so much on income as on the state-organized supply of foods and industrial consumer goods. In this respect, Romania's situation has deteriorated. A journalist for the Frankfurter Allgemeine Zeitung, Viktor Maier, commented, in his most recent report from Romania: "Since November of last year there has been a catastrophic crisis in supply in Romania (the situation is somewhat better for industrial products) the likes of which have not been seen since the Stalinist '50s. Not only meat but also dairy products, cooking oils, margarine, sugar, and quite often even bread are in short supply."[28]

## A GROWING DEBT

Romania has expanded its foreign trade relations appreciably in the last decade, especially with the industrial countries of the West and the developing countries, which has had an impact on the regional structure of foreign trade.

Development and Regional Structure

| | 1970 | | 1975 | | 1980 | |
|---|---|---|---|---|---|---|
| | Export | Import | Export | Import | Export | Import |
| Total, Millions of dollars | 1,835 | 1,953 | 5,532 | 5,532 | 12,546 | 13,540 |
| Share, percent | | | | | | |
| Socialist countries | 58.1 | 54.0 | 46.0 | 43.6 | 41.0 | 39.0 |
| OECD countries | 32.2 | 34.6 | 35.0 | 42.2 | 39.0 | 35.0 |
| Developing countries | 9.7 | 12.4 | 19.0 | 14.2 | 20.0 | 26.0 |

Source: Wochenbericht des Deutschen Institutes für Wirtschaftsforschung, 25/81.

These statistics show that both exports and imports have increased considerably. Exports to the West, however, have not been able to keep pace with imports from the West. The deficit in the balance of trade and services has increased especially in the last three years, from $0.8 billion in 1978 to $1.7 billion in 1979 and $2.4 billion in 1980. The debt has also increased accordingly in this period from $5.1 billion in 1978 to $7.2 billion in 1979 and $9.7 billion in 1980. At the end of 1980 the debt was equivalent to 1.5 years of exports to the West.

Romania and Hungary are the only East European countries that are members of the Bretton Woods institutions. Its debt to the World Bank and the International Monetary Fund was $948 million at the end of 1979.[29] Romania intends to make more use of the facilities of this institute in the future. In mid-June 1981 the International Monetary Fund granted Romania a standby credit of $1.46 million.

## REFINEMENTS WITHIN THE TRADITIONAL STEERING SYSTEM

The supply crisis has become more chronic, and the disproportions in the country's economic structures are insurmountable. Agriculture, which has been neglected for years, will be unable to achieve the yields expected of it without considerable investment. Investment resources have become scarcer, and the debt to the West has become greater.

Under the given political conditions, which the party leadership does not intend to alter, no structural economic reforms can be instituted that will reorganize the economy and promote technical progress. The party leadership is aware of this. There has never been any talk of structural reform, either at the end of the '60s, when the first signs of the crisis began to appear, or today, when the extent and destructive effects of that crisis have become unmistakable.

As in December 1967, the party decision of March 1978 projected merely a reform in planning and steering; more stress would be placed than previously on self-financing and self-maintenance of economic units. More importance was attached than before to value categories. On 1 January 1981 production prices were reviewed, and prices for fuels were brought closer to world market prices, but the reform in retail prices was postponed to 1982. Thus, consumer goods would require more state subsidies than before.

Another step toward a more rational economic accounting system was made on 1 January 1981 when the multiple exchange rate structure was replaced by a uniform exchange rate of $1.00 per 15 lei. An identical rate was also fixed for the transferable ruble, despite the fact that this had been pegged 32.5 percent higher than the dollar in early 1981 by the International Bank for Economic Cooperation. The discrepancy between the commercial rate of the leu (15 lei = $1.00) currently in force and the noncommercial rate (12 lei = $1.00) was not eliminated.

A few new tones were struck in economic policy, especially in investment activities. The investment volume of 1,350 billion lei, announced earlier for the five-year period 1981–1985, was reduced to 1,200 billion lei; the total investment rate, however, was reduced only slightly below the 40 percent mark, and its apportionment has not substantially changed. The main stress continues to be on electronics, on prospecting for and processing raw materials, and on energy and mining. Agriculture continues to be ailing; its share in total investments decreased from 13.5 percent in 1980 to 11.6 percent in 1981.

The plan for 1981 to 1985 did not alter much in the structure of industrial production; steel manufacture is to increase by 7.5 percent to 8 percent annually, and by 1985 is projected to reach 20–24 million tons. Machinery construction will probably increase by 8.8 percent average per year. The chemical industry leads the list, with a planned annual growth rate of 10.2 percent.

In view of the growing debt to the West, efforts will be made to step up exports. An increase of 75 percent, instead of the 50 percent specified in the original plan, is targeted for total turnover, to be achieved principally by stepping up exports. The course originally embarked upon of reducing foreign debt until it was "completely paid off" was abandoned as early as mid-1981, when a stand-by credit of $1.46 billion was requested from the International Monetary Fund. The real income of the population, which is at present very modest, is to increase only slightly — by 4.2–4.6 percent yearly. Romania was forced to reschedule its credit payments.

Neither technical and organizational improvements, a somewhat better set of accounting instruments, nor, finally, a few new tones in economic policy are capable of influencing, to any appreciable extent, the economic structure of the country, for a deep contradiction exists between the productive forces and the relations of production that will require more than changes merely within the existing framework of the system.

# 5

# Poland's Crisis—A Crisis of the System

"Poland's independence is a necessity for the harmonious and active coexistence of the European nations. It can be achieved only through the struggle of the young Polish proletariat, and it is well cared for in its hands. For the independence of Poland is just as necessary for the workers of all of the rest of Europe as it is for the Polish workers themselves." Thus wrote Frederick Engels on 10 February 1892 in the preface to the third Polish edition of the Manifesto of the Communist Party.[1] And indeed, the same could be written today by the same authors if they should feel inclined to venture printing a new edition of the Manifesto after what happened in Poland in 1980 and 1981.

Poland's big neighbor, and its smaller neighbors as well, rightly claim that Poland's situation is not just an internal affair of the Polish people but an international matter. The economic system prevailing today in Poland has been forced upon it.

If a few internal factors have contributed to bringing the inherent crisis of the system to such an acute pass as has happened in Poland, this is only an indication that the imported social system was, and is, least of all suited for that country. It is a banality to say that there is no one social system suited for countries that are socially and economically differently structured. No theory, least of all Marxist theory, can claim otherwise. Even Stalin knew that his form of "socialism" would be inappropriate in Poland. In 1944 he said: "To introduce communism into Poland would be like trying to put a saddle on a cow"; and he assured the Prime Minister of the Polish government in exile in London, Stanislaw Mikolajczyk, that he had no intention of imposing socialism upon the Poles because, being individualists, they would not accept a collectivist regime. Nonetheless, this is precisely what he did. Stalin's views of 1944 have retained their validity. A regime was forced upon the Poles that, from the very beginning, came into conflict with national traditions, the imperatives of economic development, and the life-style of the Polish people.

The regime reached an economic dead end at least three times: in 1956, 1970, and 1980. If it still exists today, it is certainly not due to a nationwide basic consensus, which has never existed, or to Marxist ideology, for the ideology of the overwhelming majority is Catholicism, or, even less, to the achievements of "really existing socialism" in Poland. As the chairman of the Polish Journalists Association, Stefan Bratkowski, said in a memorandum to the party leadership in March 1981: "The young Poles in Solidarity have learned to see socialism as the ideological cover for the presumption and arbitrariness of bureaucracy, propaganda, mystifications, chaos, economic voluntarism, the Byzantinism of political morals, and an ossification of structures."[2]

Like Bratkowski, Wladyslaw Markiewicz, a section director in the Academy of Sciences, also sees the causes of the crisis in the fact that "a bureaucratic model of socialism was introduced and implemented in Poland. But this model of socialism, introduced long ago, has not enabled us to move on to authentic socialism."[3]

## NATIONAL FACTORS ARE RESPONSIBLE FOR THE ACUTENESS OF THE CRISIS, BUT NOT FOR THE CRISIS ITSELF

It cannot be sufficiently stressed that the Polish crisis is not just a national phenomenon. It is a crisis of the system of the entire Eastern bloc. The manifestations of crisis may differ from country to country, and in Poland they are more acute than elsewhere. In no case has it been a question of philosophical socialism being unrealizable. The division of a society in which liberty, equality, and fraternity reign, remains a utopia however much its scientific status may be protested. The misfortune does not so much lie in the fact that the exalted promises of socialism could not be realized as in the fact that there has never been an adequate steering system. Indeed, as the *enfant terrible* of Polish journalism, Stefan Kisielewski, says: "It has turned out that the system we call socialism was suited neither to modern production relations, to the structure of an agrarian industrial nation, nor to the requirements of a democratic evolution of society."[4]

It is not only in Poland that people have rebelled against the regime prevailing in the Eastern bloc, even if discontent has been greater in that country and the popular protests more dynamic than elsewhere. There is also no statistically demonstrable evidence that the efficiency of the Polish economy, seen as a whole, is essentially less than in the other Eastern countries. If, comparatively, a few sectors of the economy are lagging behind, this is because the social system, for various reasons, has been rejected more violently. It is simply not true that Poland's economic and political crisis is a consequence of a violation of the principles of real socialism, as apologists both in Poland and in the neighboring socialist countries claim. It is rather a consequence of the zeal with which the party leadership has held fast to the principles of the regime imposed upon the country. In Poland the "leading role" of the United Polish Workers Party is firmly entrenched in the constitution. Although there are two other legal parties, namely, the Democratic Party and the People's Party, they have no right to oppositional activities, and since 1947 have not been permitted to put up their own list of candidates for parliamentary election.

The industrial enterprises are owned by the state and, as in the other East European countries, are steered centrally by the state; the state plan is law and a binding directive. Poland's economy, like the economies of the other Eastern countries, is committed to giving priority to armaments and other heavy industry. Poland is an active CMEA member and a champion of economic integration in Eastern Europe, as well as an active member of the Warsaw Pact. Furthermore, no other people in Eastern Europe has learned the commandments of geopolitics so well as have the Polish people. Never has a desire to take Poland out of the institutionalized organizations of the community been overtly stated.

The economic policy of the '70s aimed to close the technology gap not by adapting the steering system to the higher production capacities that had by then developed, but rather by means of imports of modern equipment and know-how from the West, financed with Western bank credits; but this was not just a Polish phenomenon. It was also no Polish invention to force economic growth by an overly ambitious investment rate and an inordinate use of labor power, instead of by creating conditions for improving capital and labor productivity by means of effective economic reforms.

Poland's economic and investment plans were carefully coordinated with those of the other CMEA countries, and Poland participated in joint projects on Soviet territory with long-term credits.

The isolation of the party leadership from the party base and from the population is today greater than ever before in postwar history. Just after World War II, the country, bled dry, could count on the support of some social strata in its reliance on the Soviet Union. Soviet troops had freed Poland from Hitler's rule, and many sincerely believed that the borders, now shifted further westward, could be defended only with the aid of the Soviet Union. The view was widespread that the economy, totally wrecked by war and occupation (40 percent of the national wealth had been lost, and the large cities, including the capital, lay in ruins) could be restored only in cooperation with the Soviet Union. The promise of a new economic order without capitalists and large landowners stirred great illusions, especially among the workers and the poor peasants.

The hope that a poor country such as Poland would find its fortune in socialism was expressed most clearly by Jozef Cyrankiewicz. The former socialist leader, who dissolved his party into the communist Polish Workers Party (PUWP) and had a hand in shaping the country's fate as Prime Minister up until 1970, said: "One must be a socialist because, after all, capitalism cannot be created without capital."[5]

A few specifically Polish circumstances made the existence of a totalitarian regime difficult in all aspects of social life. The ruling Communist Party had never been acknowledged as an ideological force, even after it had assumed control over all the mass media. The Catholic Church suffered many setbacks in the postwar period, owing to the destructive activities of the "patriot priests," loyal to the state, and persecution, which culminated in the isolation of Cardinal Stefan Wyszynski.

In the past two decades it has rapidly recovered, however. In 1980 the Catholic people of Poland were more Catholic than in 1945. Not only purely religious factors were responsible: the fact that the Church was the only social force able to offer resistance to the regime was also a contributing factor. The election of Wojtyla as Pope of the Catholic Church and his visit in the summer of 1979, celebrated by the entire nation, showed a despairing nation that it had status and worth beyond its mere existence as a socialist state.

The country's leading intellectuals had never supported the regime; those who did support it did not enjoy much authority among their own ranks and even less among the people.

Even measured by Eastern standards, economic policy was beset by unpardonable planning errors, especially in the Gierek era. The heavy industry model and the gigantomania assumed monstrous forms. Giant foundries and chemical combinates were built, but traditional sectors of industry, especially light industry and the foodstuffs industry, were neglected. Above all, agriculture was driven to ruin. Even after the resistance of the peasants had defeated collectivization of agriculture and the dismantling of the unviable cooperatives had become an established fact associated with Gomulka's comeback in 1956, there had never been hope that private plots, which make up three-fourths of the arable surface area and provide no less than 70 percent of agricultural products, would be maintained over the long term. They suffered discrimination vis-à-vis the state farms and received less fertilizer and farm machinery, pest-control agents, and building materials. If Poland has been transformed from a net exporter into a net importer of farm products and has never been able to overcome its supply problems, this is above all a consequence of its shortsighted agrarian policy, hostile to the peasant. Gierek's crew drew on Western credits far beyond the normal extent to finance a bankrupt economic policy and, in the end, made the country insolvent. That the Gierek regime may have been more liberal than the preceding party leaderships, that it shied away from terror, and that it gave the opposition a broad margin of freedom, especially in the second half of the '70s, may have influenced the form the mass uprising took, but it was not its cause.

Poland's path into crisis lies deeply entrenched in the contradictory history of this country. A retrospective glance will make this clearer.

## POLAND BEFORE AND AFTER WORLD WAR II

Poland began its existence as a people's republic with a considerably reduced population and a considerably reduced territory: it was compelled to cede a territory of 180,000 square kilometers, with large cities such as Lvov, Stanislawow, Tarnopol, and Vilnius, to the Soviet Union; 104,000 square kilometers of German territory was awarded to the Poles. Thus, the sovereign territory was reduced from 388,000 to 312,000 square kilometers. The population, which during the period between the wars had grown by 7 million, was reduced from 34.8 million to 23.6 million as a result of war losses, border adjustments, and resettlements.

The situation created by the economic system, which was unsuited for Poland, and the radical restructuring of foreign trade relations had a major influence on postwar development. Before the war Poland's chief trading partners were not the Eastern countries, but Germany, with a share of 24 percent, followed by Great Britain, with 15 percent, and the United States, with 10 percent.[6] In 1930 Poland imported goods valued at only 300,000 rubles from the Soviet Union, while the export volume was no more than 1.6 million rubles. The attempt to restore prewar relations with the West foundered, though its share in Poland's total foreign trade increased from 30 percent in 1946 to 61 percent in 1947. After Poland was forced to renounce participation in the Marshall Plan, the Western share in Poland's foreign trade decreased to 30 percent by 1953.[7] If one considers that the Eastern markets were just being formed at that time, it is clear that it was not easy for Poland to absorb the loss of the Western market. The terms of trade were not very favorable. Poland was neither classified as a hostile nation nor recognized as an ally. The Soviet Union made no claims on German property in Poland, but any enterprise that could be shown to have had the least ties to the armaments industry was dismantled and transported to the East. Poland was exempted from reparations, but between 1945 and 1953 had to deliver 50 million tons of coal to the Soviet Union at a price $1.25 a ton.[8] This was only a tenth of the world market price at the time. The low price was forced upon Poland only because some of those employed in Polish mines had been war prisoners. From the very beginning the country was incapable of developing an export potential that could have covered import needs: between 1951 and 1957 imports increased by 60 percent, but exports by only 6 percent.[9]

## THE HEAVY HERITAGE OF THE PREWAR PERIOD

The successes and failures of the Polish economy can be adequately evaluated only if one takes into account the grim economic history of the period between the wars and the restructuring of the territory and population after World War II.

Poland was forced to give up its energy resources (oil, coal, and wood) and the fertile lands of the rich eastern territories, and in compensation received the highly developed western territories, which, however, were not inhabited by Poles. The decisive factor for integration of the newly structured state territory was, however, not the circumstance that 20 percent of the prewar territory had been lost as a result of the border adjustments, but the fact that the western territories, which owed their high level of development to the level of civilization of the indigenous population, had to be settled with a completely alien population group from the eastern territories that had its roots in other traditions and socioeconomic structures.

Of course, the migrations brought about by the tragic events of the war and the postwar period had positive effects as well, since Poland did become a unified nation. Nevertheless, the economic and political leaderships of the country were considerably weakened by political developments.

Economically, postwar Poland had a heavy heritage to bear, not only because about 40 percent of the national wealth had been destroyed during the war but also because there had been no adequate development in the period between the wars, and because Poland's desolate economy had been especially hard hit by the world economic crisis.

The great scholar of this period Professor Zbigniew Landau pinpoints Poland's economic problems in the prewar period: "The economy of the Polish territory was embedded in alien economic and state organisms. To be sure, capitalism developed in Poland, but the attendant industrialization assumed an insular complexion that had only a minor influence on the shaping of the domestic market."[10]

With agriculture accounting for 45 percent and industrial production for only 30 percent of the national product, Poland before World War II was an agrarian country and held 16th place in the world in this respect.[11]

The national market was limited, particularly because of the extremely low purchasing power of the peasants, who made up more than half of the prewar population. More than 90 percent of the peasant plots had only an extremely negligible commodity output. The lingering economic crisis hit backward agriculture especially hard: in the years 1930 to 1935 the prices of industrial goods fell by a third, while the prices of agricultural products fell by two-thirds. Although the peasants could sell more, their earnings were lower and were scarcely enough to pay taxes and insurance. Not much remained for the purchase of industrial goods.

But the buying power of the urban population was not very high either; there were 500,000 to 1 million unemployed. Poland's industry was composed of small enterprises: of 272,500 enterprises that obtained a patent license in 1938, 242,000 (89 percent) were small businesses.[12] In the period between 1933 and 1938, the number of small businesses increased by 36 percent; the number of large firms, on the other hand, decreased from 922 to 737, i.e., by 20 percent.[13] The number of employed workers also decreased from 858,400 in 1929 to 808,400 in 1938. Three-fifths of those employed in industry were in the foundry, metal, and textile industries, located mainly in Silesia, Warsaw, and Lodz. The other regions of the country were economically extremely underdeveloped.

The number of unemployed was much higher than average, as may be seen from the following table:[14]

| | Number of employed on 30 September of each year (in millions) | | Number of unemployed on 30 September | Unemployed, in % of employed |
|---|---|---|---|---|
| | Total | In industry | | |
| 1929 | 2.40 | 0.88 | 71,000 | 2.9 |
| 1933 | 1.79 | 0.57 | 781,000 | 43.6 |
| 1936 | 2.02 | 0.71 | 619,000 | 30.6 |

It is evident from these figures that in the crisis year 1933, more than two-fifths of those able to work were unemployed. But in 1936 as well, when business was relatively good, the proportion of unemployed had declined to only about a third. On the whole, Poland's industry before the war increased only slightly; the per capita output even decreased.

The margin between the low point of the crisis and the peak of the upswing, which in countries of a similar level of development was, for example, 17 percent in Spain, 23 percent in Hungary, and 36 percent in Italy, reached 41 percent in Poland.[15]

The extreme weakness of private capital is especially important in assessing the effects of later changes in the system. The significant progress made in some areas of industry between the wars was due to state, not private, initiative. The state initiated the project of the Central Industrial Area (COP), which was to create 107,000 jobs, and participated in the financing of the Gdynia Harbor. The state share in the development of Polish industry was above average: 100 percent in aircraft and automobile construction, 55 percent in the foundry industry, and 30 percent in the machine-tool industry. The capitalist contribution was insignificant. The former director of the Polish Industrial Association "Leviathan," M. Szydlowski, described its role as follows: "Anyone asked to name a Polish capitalist of rank and renown would name Falter. But what does Falter mean in Silesia in comparison with Flick in Berlin, who rules Silesia from there?"[16]

The share of foreign capital in Poland's corporations was above average: in 1937 it was 40.1 percent — but 87.5 percent in the oil industry, 81.3 percent in electricity and water supply, 66.1 percent in the electrical engineering industry, 59.9 percent in the chemical industry, and 52.1 percent in the mining and foundry industry.[17] Capitalists as a group had hardly been able to strike roots in Poland in the period between the wars. The proportion of Catholics in the total number of firm owners was only 51.1 percent in 1931; the proportion of citizens of Jewish faith, 40.3 percent; and Protestants owned 5.5 percent of the firms.[18] In the wholesale trade, Catholics represented 28 percent, and Jews represented 53.1 percent of proprietors.[19]

In the short period of independence, 1918–1939, the most important sectors of Poland's economy, such as the chemical, electrical engineering, and armaments industries, and the infrastructure as a whole showed considerable progress. Culture, education, and the mass media developed. The number of inhabitants rose from 27.4 million in 1921 to 33.8 million in 1936. The share of the urban population in the total, however, increased from only 24 percent to 27 percent.[20]

In comparison with other countries of Europe, the social and economic structure of the country was backward. According to the 1931 census, only 39.4 percent of the population were employed outside agriculture; in Hungary at the time this figure was 43.4 percent; in Denmark, 59.3 percent; and in Germany, 65.6 percent.[21] The agrarian reform introduced immediately after independence brought only very slight improvements. Between 1919 and 1938, 2.6 million hectares were redistributed from large estates to the peasants[22]; 15,000 large farms controlled 26 percent of the land in 1935, and over half of the forest industry. Sixteen million peasants possessed 57.6 percent of the land and only 12 percent of the forest economy.[23] Agriculture was thoroughly atomized: 39.2 percent of the farms had no more than 2 hectares of arable land, and 26.3 percent had less than 5 hectares. Only a fourth of the farms (about 4 million) possessed 5–10 hectares, and only 10.5 percent, more than 10 hectares.[24]

At least 4 million peasants were superfluous in the economy and were able to leave the soil without any special harm being done to agrarian output.[25]

## NATIONALIZATION AS A MEANS OF INDUSTRIALIZATION

The war even further decimated the ranks of Polish capitalists, which had never been large in any case. The enterprises that had worked for the German armaments industry, were dismantled and transported to the East.

Under these conditions, nationalization of industrial enterprises amounted mainly to the expropriation of foreign, particularly German, large land holdings. However, not only were large firms nationalized but segments of small-scale trade as well. Even today, however, small enterprises outside agriculture employ 565,000, which is about 4 percent of the total.

Nationalization of agriculture, which affected primarily large estates of the Church and the feudal princes, could in many respects be seen as a consummation of the agrarian reform begun before the war, but subsequently left hanging. The expropriated large estates were, however, not redistributed among small peasants, but reorganized into state agrarian enterprises (PGRs). The peasant plots were to have been merged into *kolkhozy*, but the bitter resistance of the peasants made this impossible.

The efficiency of the new economic system was further reduced because the transformations, so fateful for the Polish people, had not been brought about by a mass movement, as in China or Yugoslavia, but by the unimportant Communist Party, which had been decimated by Stalin's purges, dissolved in 1938, and restored in 1942, and become the ruling party through the will of the *force majeur*.[26]

The priority this system gave to political reliability over specialized skills, especially in the first phase of development, was not conducive to good economic management. The number of scientific and technical specialists from the *ancien régime* who had been expelled and, correspondingly, the number of unskilled, but politically reliable, managers was necessarily very high.[27] The forced structural change gave rise to major economic and political contradictions that those in power tried to resolve using the violent methods typical of the Stalinist style of government. Among the victims were, as everywhere else, the children of the imported revolution, especially the party leader Gomulka and Spychalski, who was later to become president of the state. The same destiny as that of Slansky and his companions was contemplated for them — Spychalski was even freighted off to Prague — but, fortunately, in Poland those in power shied away from show trials and death sentences.

## THE *STURM UND DRANG* PERIOD FROM 1946 TO 1955; 1956 TOTALLY DISCREDITED

The idealism of the pioneers and the belief of a large segment of the workers that a just social system would follow the liberation from long years of occupation, the concentrated effort of the people to undo the damage caused by the war as fast as possible, to rebuild the devastated cities, and to set the wrecked economy in motion once again made the initial postwar period the most successful in Poland's economic history.

The new Polish version of the Soviet NEP model did indeed manage to restore Poland's prewar potential: A significant portion of industrial enterprises, especially small businesses and domestic trade, were in private hands, central planning was still *in statu nascendi*, and economic mechanisms still played some role. In 1945 industrial production was 30 percent lower than in 1939; but by 1946, it had risen by 30 percent, to only 6.8 percent below the prewar level.[28]

From the very beginning, however, agriculture was extremely backward, and in 1947 achieved only half of the prewar output. Supply problems were alleviated by UNRRA deliveries, which accounted for 79 percent of total imports in the first half of 1946 and 45 percent in the second half; thanks to these, total imports in 1946 were 57 percent greater than in 1938, while exports were only at one-third the prewar volume.[29]

In 1949 industrial output was 48 percent, and the national product 25 percent, above the prewar level; but agriculture was still 10 percent below it.

Even by this time the negative effects of a dynamic but disproportionate economic growth were already becoming apparent, with a massive investment of capital and labor, producing major discrepancies between supply and demand. Industrial output, driven forward by huge capital outlays, as agriculture lagged and the share of UNRRA imports in total imports fell to 21 percent in the first half-year of 1947,[30] pushed prices skyward. By the end of 1948 they were 47.7 percent higher than in April 1945. At that time an attempt was made to restore equilibrium through further nationalizations and state controls. The share of nationalized trade in total retail trade increased between 1947 and 1950 by 29 percent, to 80 percent; in 1948 the price rises were curbed somewhat. Total nationalization of industrial enterprises and nationalization of trade and the replacement of economic mechanisms by central planning and administration created the preconditions for an arbitrary economic policy by means of which inflated capital investments made an inordinate growth of heavy industry possible at the expense of agriculture and the consumer goods industry, initially with domestic, and later with increasingly more Western, credits. This was the economic policy responsible for every development phase's — 1945–1956, 1957–1970, and 1970–1980 — ending in a serious crisis.

In 1950 the NEP period came to an end. The six-year plan, especially the 1951 version corrected by the Soviet Union, produced a pace and structure of growth that in many respects resembled the first five-year plan of the Soviet Union. Industrial output increased by 2.7 times, 15 percent more rapidly than targeted in the plan; the national product, on the other hand, grew by only 90 percent, and the discrepancy in the growth rates of these two economic areas was ascribed to the backwardness of agriculture, which the attempt to collectivize had damaged immeasurably. Agriculture grew by 13 percent, from an initial level that was already low, with grain crops increasing by only 2.6 percent.[31]

Many large enterprises were constructed during the period of the plan. However, the disproportions merely grew, since the principal factor in industrial growth was a tremendous investment of capital and labor, the consequence of which was an increase in buying power so great that it could not be covered by the supply of consumer goods. Inventories increased fourfold, but not of goods that could have met the needs of the people and of industry.

The share of investments in the national product increased from 22.7 percent in 1949 to 29.4 percent in 1950 and 38.2 percent in 1953, and then, as a result of the severe crisis in supply, decreased in the last 2 years of the six-year plan by 32.8 percent and 31.2 percent, respectively.[32] The share of consumption in the above-average increase in the national product in the years 1952 and 1953 was no more than 20 percent and 24 percent, respectively: in the 6 years between 1950 and 1955, real wages increased by only 13 percent.[33]

The consequences of this dynamic but chaotic growth were devastating. To reduce the inflated buying power without a commensurate growth in supply, it was necessary to undertake two comprehensive measures in the course of the six-year plan.

On 28 October 1950, a currency and price reform was instituted, for the second time since the end of the war: the money in circulation was exchanged against new money at a 100:1 ratio, and prices and wages were converted at a ratio of 100:3. Despite the fact that the currency reform of October 1950 reduced the volume of money by one-third, in 1951 and 1952 new signs of a market inflation appeared because of the disproportionate economic growth; between 1951 and 1953, the retail price index increased by 97 percent. At the beginning of 1953 the government felt itself compelled to implement a new price and wages reform. Wages were increased by 30 percent, but prices by 40 percent.

The Polish economic expert Professor M. Kucharski described the economic policy introduced during the six-year plan as follows: "Stress was laid on heavy industry, i.e., on sectors with an above-average production cycle and a complicated supply structure.... The economic policy was marked by an exaggerated optimism and the assumption that a high volume of investment was compatible with a high income of the population."[34] This applied to the Gomulka, and even more to the Gierek, era of the '70s.

An attempt was made, in vain, to embark on an independent course in economic development. Private initiative was to be more actively enlisted, and enterprises were not to be so tightly bound to central directives; the traditional sectors of the economy, the textiles and foodstuffs industries, were to be given greater consideration. Nothing came of all of this. The six-year plan between 1948 and 1953, which was crucial to the further economic growth of Poland, was adjusted by the *force majeure*, and the stress was laid on heavy industry. The Korean War was also a factor.

The management of heavy industry and the armaments industry developed into an extremely powerful pressure group over the course of time, which often diverted to itself, against the will of the central leadership, more investment funds than the nation's economy could afford. The consumer goods industry remained underdeveloped. Hidden inflation and permanent undersupply were the principal causes of the growing signs of discontent among the population.

When work norms were raised once more, the Polish people lost patience. The workers' uprising in Poznan clearly showed that the economic and political system of Poland had entered a serious crisis.

## THE GREAT HOPE: GOMULKA'S COMEBACK, OCTOBER 1956; BANKRUPT IN DECEMBER 1970

Wladyslaw Gomulka, the martyr of the Stalinist phase in Poland, arrested in 1949 for "nationalist deviation," returned to power in the "Polish October" (1956), celebrated by the entire people. When in late 1956 he returned from Moscow with annulment of the Polish debt as a return favor for the coal and meat deliveries Poland had made at symbolic prices, the enthusiasm was so great that he was lifted from the ground, together with his automobile, by the rejoicing people.

Gomulka had come to power against the will of the Soviet Union. Khrushchev had come to Warsaw accompanied by three Politburo members to prevent Gomulka's impending appointment as First Secretary of the Polish United Workers Party. An invasion of Soviet troops was feared then as well. Remarkably, the American government, as was not the case with regard to Hungary (1956) and Czechoslovakia (1968), was ready for counteraction. In a Pentagon document (JCS 2066/19) we may read: "If the Soviet Union employs military means to suppress the new Polish regime, and if the new Polish government resists and directs a prompt request to the UN, the United States will call, and be prepared, for every appropriate U.S. action, including the use of force, that is necessary to prevent the USSR from successfully restoring its control by violence."[35] The Soviet Union did not send in its troops. It resigned itself to the fact that its generals, with Marshal Rokossovskii at the head, and many other advisers had to return to the Soviet homeland.

Gomulka returned to the Soviet fold gradually as he reverted to the old methods of government and the traditional economic policy. Khrushchev and Brezhnev regarded him as a good personal friend and as a friend of the Soviet Union as well. In December 1970 he was allowed to fall, just as his successor was to be allowed to fall in August 1980.

Gomulka had a unique historical opportunity to exert a decisive influence on the history of his homeland, and perhaps on that of the entire Eastern community. In his first years in government it seemed that he would make use of this opportunity. Most of the *kolkhozy*, hated by the peasants, were dissolved. Within a few months their number decreased from 10,600 to 1,700; their share in Polish agricultural production fell to no more than 2.5 percent. The Economic Council created under the chairmanship of Oskar Lange drew up promising proposals for reorganizing the economy and improving the steering system; decentralization of economic powers and far-reaching rights for the workers' councils were his principal goals.

Unlike his Hungarian colleague Kadar, however, Gomulka did not make use of his historical opportunity. Faced with the alternatives of basing his domestic power and the country's economic policy either on liberal politicians and the masses or on the hard-liners in the party apparatus, he chose the latter. The liberals were forced to resign, one after the other: Matwin, Morawski, Albrecht, Rapacki, and many others.

The components of the 1956 reform program were allowed to fall by the wayside one by one; the bodies of self-administration for factory workers, formed spontaneously in the first phases of the Gomulka era, were merged into a unified body of the trade union, workers' self-determination councils, and a party committee (the SKR), under the leadership of the party. Thus, the traditional centrally administered system was gradually restored.

Economic growth was driven forward by the traditional methods, i.e., inflated investment of capital and labor. The share of accumulation in the national product, which had fallen from 38.2 percent in 1953 to 32.8 percent and 31.2 percent, respectively, in the next 2 years of the 7-year plan, in 1965 once again reached a level of 36.2 percent (1961 prices).[36] The share of individual consumption fell from 68 percent to 64.1 percent in 1965 and 61.9 percent in 1970.[37] Labor productivity in industry increased by 32 percent in the first half of the '60s, but by only 24 percent in the second half.[38]

In the '70s many enterprises were built, the raw materials and energy base was expanded, and jobs were created for 1.5 million people. Economic growth, however, became more expensive: in the second half of the '60s, the national income increased by 34 percent but investment expenditure increased by 50 percent. The investment rose from a 7 percent annual average rate in the first half of the '70s to 8.5 percent in the second half. The pace was greater than in the USSR, the GDR, and Czechoslovakia. It was a progress, however, that was accompanied by no perceptible improvement in the material situation of the employed. Production grew rapidly, and consumption, slowly, as was stated at the Plenary Session of the Central Committee of the party in February 1971, after the fall of the Gomulka leadership.

Once again, as in the mid-'50s, by the end of the '60s the economic-political system of the country had reached a complete dead end. Agriculture, with an annual growth rate of 1.8 percent, showed an especially poor performance; it was increasingly becoming the Achilles heel of the nation's economy. Wages and salaries increased at an almost imperceptible rate of 1.7 percent a year.

Political and social conflicts reached their peak in the spring of 1968, with a rebellion of the youth and the intellectuals. It was not until two years later that the workers raised their might voice.

A strong group of former partisans, led by the then Minister of the Interior, Moczar, attempted to take advantage of the growing political confusion and to seize the power that had slipped from the political leadership into their own hands with superpatriotic and anti-Semitic slogans.

Gomulka attempted to intimidate the youth and intellectuals with mass terror. Nor was he reluctant to participate in the defeat of the Prague Spring in August 1968, to knock the ground from under "socialism with a human face" in Poland. To take the wind from Moczar's sails, he permitted a total purge of Jews from the political and economic apparatus. Almost all the Jews emigrated, the third wave of emigrants in Poland's postwar history. But the economic problems persisted.

The Gomulka era rapidly approached its bitter end. When Gomulka tried to relieve the broad disparity between supply and demand, once again by the usual means, i.e., through drastic price rises that would have reduced the already negligible rise in incomes to nothing — moreover, just before Christmas (1970) — the Poles had had enough. The workers' uprising unseated the leader of the Workers Party and his retinue and no one in the country shed tears for the once highly acclaimed leader.

The crisis that accompanied the end of Gomulka's rule differed notably from the one that had helped him in his comeback. In 1956 the regime was only ten years old. At that time the crisis itself, like the personality cult in the Soviet Union, could be interpreted as a "plant accident" and a "deformation" of the principles of socialism instead of as an inevitable consequence of real socialism, despite the fine-sounding words with which it was masked.

As in the "Prague Spring" of 1968, the events in Poland in 1956 were more a matter of revolt within the party apparatus than a mass uprising. The party apparatus, divided into two factions, "Natolin," the dogmatists, and "Pulaska," the liberals, put a man at their head who could be seen as a symbol of resistance against the Stalinist regime and who was capable of uniting the programs of the two clashing factions under an anti-Stalinist roof. As a martyr of the Stalinist regime, Gomulka was not only the right leader for the party apparatus, he was also acceptable to the majority of the people.

In December 1970 the regime was 25 years old. An economic and political crisis was shaking the country after 14 years of unlimited power in the hands of the same man to whom the country had given a full vote of confidence in 1956. In 1970 he was but a mere shadow of his former self. He and his followers had totally exhausted themselves in the exercise of power, depleted the potential of talent, and isolated themselves from the people and the party base. The illusion that a humane socialism could be built under his leadership had totally faded away.

The regime had come to a dead end. The resistance movement was strong, however, but different from that of 1980. It was spontaneous and unorganized. It lacked a conscious and purposeful leadership. The unorganized rebellion of the workers, isolated from the other strata of the population (the students and intellectuals had rebelled in 1968, without support from the workers), was incapable of putting through any institutional changes that might have prevented a renewal of the dictatorial methods of rule. But the rebellion was much more massive and dangerous than in 1956. For the first time in the history of Eastern Europe, a mass movement was able to bring down a party leadership. The strikes and mass demonstrations that began on the Baltic seacoast spread like wildfire to other areas of the country: on 19 December 100 firms in 7 of the 19 Woiwodships struck; according to official figures, the unrest claimed 45 dead and 1,965 wounded. Nineteen state buildings were burned, including the building of the party committee of Gdansk and Szczecin. Two hundred and twenty shops were destroyed. Between 14 and 20 December 1970, 2,989 persons were arrested.[39]

It was not the weak heart that his physicians had diagnosed that cast Wladyslaw Gomulka, in December 1970, and his successors ten years later, into political oblivion. Both personified the political illness of a social order that Gomulka was supposed to have cured of the miseries of the Stalinist period and Gierek of the miseries of the Gomulka era: the incurable disease of a one-party regime and a centrally steered economy controlled by that regime, which, because of a lack of economic mechanisms, was uncontrollable and exposed to the arbitrary whims of any party leader. Its defeat was the defeat of a political power that had become intolerable, but that continued to exist because of a superpower that limited the sovereignty of the people.

In 1970 Edward Gierek was able to bring the situation under control without altering any institutions in the exercise of power, but if he succeeded in doing this, it was more because of the circumstance that at that time there was no politically formed and conscious opposition than because of his qualities as a politician or an economist. The workers, who had long since realized that the Polish United Workers Party represented the interests of the political and economic bureaucracy rather than their interests, were not prepared to form their own autonomous common-interest groups. Any alternative to the universally hated Gomulka regime was acceptable to them. Gierek was at that time the strongest man in the party apparatus and was, moreover, able to gain the support of the most important opponent of Gomulka, the former partisan leader M. Moczar. He sharply criticized the methods of power of the overthrown leader and promised much, among other things to build a "second Poland," and once again, like his predecessor in 1956, to put the needs of the people foremost in his economic policy.

The fact that Gierek's criticism of his predecessor could be applied to himself ten years later, and in much sharper terms, shows more clearly than anything else that the assumption that the economic and political crisis of 1980 was a crisis of the system, not a cyclical crisis, is correct. In 1980 the regime was already 35 years old, the crisis was deeper, and the disappointment and disillusionment of the population were much greater than in 1956 and 1970.

When Gierek assumed the role of successor to Gomulka, he was quite aware of the diagnosis of the country's political illness. The Eighth Plenary Session of the Central Committee in February 1971 observed: "The crisis of confidence, which extends over many strata, is the most essential expression of the deep contradiction between the new production capacities and the level of civilization of Poland, on the one hand, and the steering methods of party and state, on the other, which are no longer commensurate with the level and needs of the present stage." Gierek also knew under what conditions such a deep crisis could arise. The same Plenary Session of the Central Committee described the fateful style of government of the overthrown leader quite trenchantly:

> No serious scientific analysis was made before economic or political decisions were taken, and experts were very rarely asked to evaluate and assess these decisions.... Political and economic decisions were made on the basis of fragmentary and quite incidental information, intuitively and arbitrarily, often inspired by self-certainty.... Within the Politburo a small group, favored by the First Secretary, had crystallized and had assumed all the reins of power for itself, suffered no criticism and tolerated no initiative, and listened only to its own voice.[40]

Nonetheless, the same methods of leadership were continued unchanged into the next decade.

The experiences of the '70s accelerated the maturation of the resistance movement; the broad strata of the population who raised their voices in 1980 no longer trusted these reshufflings among the party leadership, nor changes in statutes. The influence of trade unions that defended the interests of the workers was reduced to an absolute minimum. Poland's working class no longer wanted trade unions that functioned as "transmission belts between the party and the employed." They wanted no privileges, but authentic unions to defend the interests of the workers in their struggle against the state bureaucracy.

## THE RAPID RISE AND DISASTER OF THE ECONOMIC POLICY — THE CHAOTIC GROWTH IN THE FIRST HALF OF THE '70S

From the very beginning, Gierek was under severe pressure. He reversed the price rises and promised to maintain stable prices, to fuel the economy, which had been stagnating since the end of the '60s, and to raise wages drastically.

The opening to the West, which the new party leadership undertook in the '70s, created the prerequisites for dynamic economic growth: whereas in 1961–1970 the national product increased by an annual average of 6.1 percent, between 1971 and 1975 the average annual growth rate was 9.8 percent. Industrial output, with an average growth rate of 10.5 percent, displayed especially dynamic development. The dynamic growth was due primarily to an active investment policy: investments increased by an annual average of 18.4 percent in the first five years of the '70s compared with 7.4 percent in the '60s.

Agriculture, however, could not keep pace with the growth in industrial output. After the years of abundance in 1972 and 1973, in which agricultural production increased by 8.4 percent and 7.3 percent, respectively, in 1974 its growth rate was only 1.6 percent. In 1975 it showed a decline of 2.3 percent, and no improvement ensued. The above-average growth placed excessive strain on resources: investment was very intensive, and hence a relatively narrow margin remained for consumption. More was distributed than could be produced. In 1960 the share of investments in the national product was 23.1 percent, in 1970 it was 26.1 percent, but in the 2 boom years 1974 and 1975, it was 36 percent and 35.2 percent. Thus, Poland showed the highest proportion of investments in national product not only in the whole of Europe but also in the extremely investment-oriented CMEA.

But the efforts of the Polish people were not sufficient to bring about this tremendous upswing. The above-average growth rate had to be financed at least partly with foreign credits. In the period from 1972 to 1976 alone, 230 billion more zlotys were distributed than produced; the foreign trade deficit with the West reached $10.2 billion during this period.

It should be noted that the economic boom in the first half of the '70s was not financed by foreign credits alone: it was also partly sustained by inflated buying power. This, however, was not matched by a commodity structure commensurate with the needs of the population, since the heavy-industry model continued to dominate the economic policy of the country even in the boom years. From 1970 to 1976 the money holdings of the population increased from 173 to 486 billion zlotys; the share of savings deposits increased from 66 percent to 70 percent. But the scarcity of consumer goods became more and more acute. Savings were forced, not voluntary. The supply problems had already become acute by the mid-'70s.

The dynamic growth in the first half of the '70s was also undoubtedly fueled by the circumstance that the ossified cells within the economic and political apparatus had loosened somewhat, much fresh air had been pumped into the shaky economy, and many economic managers had been replaced by younger and more talented ones. Yet in the same process in which the style of leadership of the new team reverted to the traditional channels of a one-party regime, the fresh atmosphere soon dissipated rapidly once more. Newly emerged and reinforced old pressure groups exercised a fatal influence on the further course of economic development.

In the second half of the Gierek era, the same characteristic features of the later "real socialism" appeared; they differ from the features of late capitalism, but are no less rife with crisis. A feature of later real socialism is the emergence of powerful branch empires that, by dint of merger of their managements with the management of the central apparatus and by dint of the institutionalized priority given to heavy industry and the armaments industry, are able to implement every decision at the expense of other branches. It is just these empires that bear the principal blame for the acute disproportionalities that threw the economy in disarray in the last years of the Gierek era and plunged it into a severe crisis. Despite the chronic scarcity of resources, they were always able to attract the largest quantities of investment funds and scarce raw and other materials.

Once foreign trade relationships with the West had been expanded, these empires took advantage of the opportunity to seal every gap in supply with imports, thus covering up every failure without being particularly concerned about expanding the range of exportable goods proportionally. The extremely powerful branch empires had created a situation in which imports had reached a volume that could no longer be financed with exports. The extremely favorable production and sales conditions that had been created exclusively for them were not sufficient to spur them to the production of high-quality goods. The demand of a competitive market is always greater than that of the sellers' market of a planned economy. The latter's criterion of success was investment in new capacities, which, whenever possible, were to be equipped with modern, i.e., imported, technology, but were seldom inclined to undertake modernization of existing production potential. It was sufficient to come into the state plan with merely a million to activate investments totaling billions. The Ninth Party Congress (July 1981) bluntly states: "The decision-making procedure was sometimes criminal; various pressure groups and coteries exercised the decisive influence."[41]

The former vice-director of the Central Planning Authorities, Józef Pajestka, said, quite rightly, that Poland's economy was planned, but did not follow the plan. So it was in the first half of the '70s, when Pajestka was still in charge of planning and a growth rate was set into motion, without consideration of existing resources, and mainly with foreign monies; and so it was also in the second half of the decade, when a chaotic retreat was instituted.

Of course, no one had planned the exorbitantly high growth rates that were achieved in the first half of the '70s. The opening of the country to Western imports and Western money had the effect that, following a cooling-off period at the end of the '60s, the economy stormed ahead again: the national product increased by 62 percent from 1971 to 1975, although the plan had targeted only 39 percent. Industrial output increased by 73 percent, 23 percentage points more than planned. Investments showed the sharpest increase, 132 percent, compared with a planned 45 percent.

It was this dynamic and chaotic investment drive, especially in heavy industry and mining, with a long-term construction cycle and a considerable import input (although many projects could not be finished on time), that led to the tremendous discrepancies and payment difficulties, which will not be brought under control for a long time yet. In 1971 Poland's trade balance was positive; but in the following years imports increased, especially from the West, much more rapidly than exports. In the period from 1971 to 1975 the annual average increase in exports was 10.7 percent, with exports to the West increasing by 8.4 percent. Imports, on the other hand, showed the reverse tendency: the total increase annually averaged 15.2 percent, while imports from the West increased by 26.4 percent.

## THE ECONOMIC REFORM CURBED

The party leadership that came to power after the stormy December days of 1970 cannot be reproached for wanting to bring the economy, which had stagnated in the late '60s, to life again, and for raising Western credits to do this, even if on too great a scale. Growth fetishism had always been great in the planned economies. The fault lay primarily in economic policy, which did not use the foreign credits and the improved political climate to further efficiency, increase labor productivity, improve the quality of goods, and produce items that would have had better sale possibilities in Westtern markets. The economic reform initiated at the beginning of the '70s came to a halt. The Polish economist Professor J. Gościński observed: "Poland entered into a phase of successive depletion of extensive production factors, a phase in which the economy opened increasingly outward, in which cooperative projects with other countries were intensified and joint ventures were begun even with non-socialist countries. But despite a few efforts at reform, the steering system remained essentially unchanged."[42]

Poland was the first country in Eastern Europe to have undertaken economic reforms as early as 1956. Interesting proposals were worked out by the ad hoc Economic Council under the direction of the well-known economist Oskar Lange. The principal aim was a debureaucratization of planning and steering. The planning committee was to be transformed from a superministry that planned and supervised every detail of economic activity into a body that concentrated mainly on long-term development models and used progressive steering methods. The enterprises were to be transformed from units that implemented the state plan into enterprises that financed themselves and received no subsidies from the state. Profit was to be made a criterion for evaluating efficiency and a means of financing enterprise growth. Prices were to be measures of performance, correspond to the value of the goods produced, and be pegged to world prices.

One of the most important components of the reformed economic system was to be workers' control bodies that were to have a voice in economic activity, together with enterprise administration.

Subsequent developments have shown, however, that a radical economic reform, or at least implementation of the most important components of such a reform, could take place only in a liberalized and debureaucratized system. Nevertheless, the Gomulka regime gradually returned to traditional administrative methods. This retreat reduced the ideas of economic reform to nothing.

Two more attempts were made, in 1964 and 1968, to reform the ossified economic system, without any success. The new leadership that came to power in late 1970 contemplated a much more modest reform. The economy was henceforth to be led by large concerns (WOGs). They were given far-ranging decision-making powers with regard to investment activities, employment, and wages. Investments were to be financed through bank credits rather than budget subsidies. This mode of financing was used in 1970 and in association with this, the investment bank was merged with the national bank in early 1970.

The principal indicators of the economic plan were to be the creation of value and the sale of goods. Wages were to be set in relation to the increase in labor productivity, in a proportion established from above.

The reform was initially tested in 28 large enterprises with a 20 percent share in total industrial output in mid-1972. Later the new steering methods were extended to 110 large concerns with a 65 percent share in industrial output.

After three years, the brakes had to be applied, because the economy had gotten out of control. Somewhat later the economic reform was totally abandoned. It must be stressed that Gierek's reform was much more modest than that of his predecessor. The father of the latter reform, Oskar Lange, wanted to delegate decision-making powers to the microlevel and give the workers an effective right of codetermination. Gierek's team, on the other hand, aspired to form large concerns and grant them certain decision-making powers, while leaving the self-determination rights in the rudimentary form in which they had found it. Under these circumstances, the large concerns, free from any pressure from below, were more willing to share their powers with the central authorities than with the enterprises.

A similar experiment failed in the GDR: in January 1963 the Sixth Party Congress of the SED decided to introduce a new economic system that granted the industrial associations (VVBs) far-ranging decision-making powers. The Fourteenth Session of the Central Committee, in December 1970, rescinded these powers almost entirely.

In Poland there was no party or government decision that rescinded the reforms introduced in the early '70s; they simply lost all their efficacy because the central authorities and the management of the most important sectors of industry, confronted with growing disproportionalities and supply problems, assumed all decision-making powers themselves. The experiences of the '70s once again showed clearly that a one-party regime has no confidence in decentralized management. If it is introduced, it is always under pressure; if difficulties occur, the reforms, half-hearted as they are, are rescinded.

## ECONOMIC MANEUVERING, OR HOW AN ALLIGATOR IS REDUCED TO THE SIZE OF A LIZARD

The two parts of this heading, the one from a party decision, the second from a popular proverb, refer to the 1976 economic policy. They can be summed up in the catch phrase, "Forward, we must retreat."

That is the way things stood in June 1976. In the first half of the '70s, when efforts had been made to remedy the disproportions that had arisen, i.e., to cancel the growth in income that had accrued to the population in this five-year period by above-average price rises (a 50 percent rise in the price of meat and meat products), the people rejected the attempt. Mass demonstrations forced the government to rescind the price rises that had already been decreed.

The government had no recourse left other than to abandon the dynamic but disproportional growth. The poorly managed dynamic growth of the first half of the '70s gave way to a chaotic retreat. The economy no longer had the steam necessary to fulfill the plan, even after a downward adjustment. The growth rates fell rapidly, as may be seen from the following statistics.

Average Annual Changes, in Percent

| | Plan | | Plan fulfillment | | | | | |
|---|---|---|---|---|---|---|---|---|
| | 1971 to 1975 | 1976 to 1980 | 1976 | 1977 | 1978 | 1979 | 1980 | 1976 to 1980 |
| Produced national income | 9.7 | 7.0–7.3 | 7.1 | 5.0 | 2.8 | –2.0 | –4.0 | 1.6 |
| Industrial output (turnover since 1977) | 10.5 | 8.2–8.5 | 9.8 | 8.6 | 5.9 | 2.8 | –1.3 | 4.3 |
| Gross output of agriculture | 3.6 | 3.2–3.5 | –0.7 | 0.8 | 4.3 | –1.4 | –9.6 | –1.5 |
| Gross investment | 18.4 | 0.2 | 2.3 | 4.3 | 1.6 | –7.0 | –9.5 | –2.3 |
| Foreign trade | | | | | | | | |
| Total imports | 23.7 | 4.6 | 10.6 | 5.5 | 4.9 | 6.3 | 6.1 | |
| from the West | 40.7 | | 9.7 | –0.7 | –1.9 | –0.2 | 0.4 | 11.2 |
| Total exports | 19.3 | 11.8 | 7.1 | 11.4 | 9.7 | 12.2 | 3.4 | |
| to the West | 11.2 | | 8.8 | 8.8 | 9.8 | 11.7 | 17.1 | 0.1 |

Sources: Rocznik Statystyczny and WIFO Monatsbericht, 4/1981, pp. 233 and 236.

So long as any supply and financing gaps could be filled by Western imports and Western credits, there was no need to curb economic growth. After all, importing economic units never felt the burden of the growing debt and debt services, and hence did not have to undertake any corrective adaptative measures. Indeed, the principal weakness of a centrally administered economy lies in the fact that central bodies do the planning and administering, but also bear the total responsibility for the economy. In the middle of the '70s, however, this burden had become too great to bear. The discrepancy between the buying power created in the years of disproportional growth and the quite meager supply of basic foods and industrial consumer goods had become intolerable.

The population had never been truthfully informed of the state of the economy: the size of the foreign debt was a closely guarded state secret. Even officials within the economy were forced to rely on foreign sources. No one believed in the propaganda of success, and no one was inclined to measure economic success in terms of the number of newly created coal mines or steel and cement capacities. The supply of basic foodstuffs collapsed in 1976, but meat and meat products continued to be exported. In 1976 the value of exported food was 2,691.2 million foreign-exchange zlotys ($890 million), including 883 million foreign exchange zlotys ($294 million) for meat and meat products.[43] It is therefore no wonder that the people rejected the attempt to shift the burden of the failed economic policy onto their shoulders through drastic price rises. Although the price rises of June 1976 were rescinded, the confidence of the ruled in the rulers was never again restored.

Growth in industrial output and investments was curbed. Imports, especially from the West, were cut back, perhaps too drastically, since at the end of 1975 Poland's foreign debt was no more than $7.4 billion, and trade with the CMEA countries still showed a positive balance in 1976 of 158 million foreign-exchange zlotys (about $500 million).[44]

Since the capacities created in the first half of the '70s were extremely import-intensive, the cutbacks in imports gave rise to new disparities. Acute bottlenecks occurred, especially in the supply of energy. Throughout the entire second half of the '70s, it proved impossible to reach a balance in trade with the West, to say nothing of the balance of payments. Interest alone consumed $1.5–2 billion in the last few years. The supply situation deteriorated perceptibly, one of the reasons being the catastrophic situation in agriculture. Although in the past five years 34 million tons of grain and 6.5 million tons of fodder had already been imported,[45] meat, sugar, and the like were rationed. There was no longer anything to prevent the deepening economic crisis from becoming a political crisis as well. Gierek's fallen team had left two giant mountains of debt behind it: about $24 billion abroad, i.e., about 730 billion zlotys, and an inflation gap that, according to cautious estimates, had reached 300 billion zlotys by the end of 1980, and would reach 1,000 billion zlotys by the end of 1985.

## THREE SOURCES OF THE CRISIS IN THE SYSTEM

### Chaotic Investment Patterns

No other area in a planned economy more graphically illustrates the contradiction between the level of development achieved and the steering mechanism, with the limits placed on it by the system, as crassly as the overinflated and disproportionate investment activity. Though this contradiction is manifest more acutely in Poland than elsewhere, it would be quite wrong to see the failures in this area as a special case, not as a typical feature of a planned economy. Every planned economy tends toward excessive investments. These are the most effective stopgaps and ways out of any emergency. The volume of investment is relatively larger than in a market economy, as is evident in the greater share of accumulation in the national product.

But the times are past in which an above-average accumulation rate was accompanied by an above-average growth rate. The long years of emphasis on extensive factors made the economy more capital-intensive than a market economy. Concentration of investment capital in heavy industry and the armaments industry, while other areas of the economy, especially housing construction, the infrastructure, and agriculture, are constantly neglected, is another symptom that is hardly typical of Poland's economy alone. As the privileged industrial branches developed into powerful pressure groups in the later development phase of real socialism, the one-sidedness of investment activities and the disproportionate growth that it caused have been revealed as an invariable factor of any planned economy. This tendency deepens the gap between politically motivated decisions at the macrolevel and the everyday practice of enterprises, while the central authorities are increasingly less able to control the growing pressure on the state resources. The consequence of this development is an excessive dispersion of investment projects and a broad construction front, an above-average number of incompleted projects, and the paradox that the industrial enterprises in the planned economies, so fearful of innovation, are, on the other hand, the most capital-intensive in the world. In a centrally administered planned economy, an enterprise receives its investment funds from the state. It is therefore not surprising that the demand for allocations of investment funds exceeds the state's means. But what is cheap for an enterprise is increasingly expensive for the society and its citizens.

In the later phase of real socialism the centrally steered, planned economy is transformed into its opposite as the centrifugal forces formed in its womb disintegrate and disorganize the structure of the planned economy, making it the most expensive economic system in the world. This expansion of disintegrating, capital-consuming factors, while resources grow increasingly more scarce, is the most essential feature of the systemic crisis in any planned economy, above all of the crisis in Poland.

However paradoxical it may sound, it can be demonstrated that the irregularities in the investment pattern, with their devastating effect on the economy, i.e., the acceleration of investments at the beginning and a slowing down of investments in the later phase of development, make the production process in a planned economy more chaotic than that of any market economy.

There were four phases in Poland's postwar history that illustrate the irregularities in the investment cycle especially clearly.

Investment Cycles in the Period between 1950 and 1980*
Annual Average Growth Rates, in Percent

| 1950 to 1957 | | 1958 to 1964 | | 1965 to 1971 | | 1972 to 1980 | |
|---|---|---|---|---|---|---|---|
| Acceleration | Slowing | Acceleration | Slowing | Acceleration | Slowing | Acceleration | Slowing |
| 1950 to 1953 | 1954 to 1957 | 1958 to 1962 | 1963 to 1964 | 1965 to 1969 | 1970 to 1971 | 1972 to 1975 | 1976 to 1980 |
| 20.4 | 5.3 | 9.9 | 3.7 | 9.2 | 5.8 | 21.3 | -2.3 |

*See P. Dziewulski and A. Maciejewski, "Nieregularnosci i ekspansja dzialalnosci inwestycyjnej," in Gospodarka Planova, 4/1980, p. 219.

The more intensive the investments were in the first phase, the more they shrank in the next phase. The data in the table show that the investment boom in the period 1972 to 1975 was even greater than in the Sturm-und-Drang period at the beginning of the '50s. The slowdown, however, was also much more drastic: an annual growth rate of 21.3 percent in the first half of the '70s was followed by a 2.3 percent decline in investments.

The decline in investment activity was an inevitable consequence of the disproportions that occurred in the acceleration phase, especially of the excessive strain placed on economic possibilities. The latter were always overstrained because no economic unit would willingly forgo the easiest and cheapest growth factor, which in a planned economy is always the investment capital allocated from the state budget. Cutbacks had to be made because the economy was no longer capable of bearing the burden of the inordinate investment activity, while at the same time access to Western credits became increasingly more difficult. Nevertheless, above all, the acute disproportions had to be reduced. A large part of investment funds were channeled into heavy industry, while the consumer-goods industry received a steadily declining share of total investments: from 35.5 percent in 1973, to 31.8 percent in 1974, 28.5 percent in 1975, and 25.5 percent in 1976.[46]

Józef Pajestka, who had been vice-director of the Polish Planning Commission for many years, justly observed that "investment activities had often and almost periodically been excessive in the country's development."[47] The present vice-director of the planning board, A. Karpiński, called the widely dispersed investments the "most expensive of generally known industrialization models, which lays claim to tremendous investment funds and demands sacrifices from the population."[48]

Statistics from the Polish National Bank and data from the most important investors show how huge the dispersion of investment projects had become: the estimated value of the 10,000 investment projects continuing into 1980 was 1,750 billion zlotys, which is only 10 percent lower than the national product in 1979 (1,935.4 billion zlotys).[49] Completion of investment projects in progress will require no less than 1.3 trillion zlotys (in 1978 prices),[50] and then only if the planned cost estimates are not exceeded, which is unlikely, judging from previous practice.

The investment projects begun in the last few years are, however, less export-oriented and less productive than earlier ones; their completion will therefore hardly be able to mitigate the country's serious situation, according to the Polish economist Jan Macieja.[51] They are extremely capital-intensive: an investment expenditure of 2.27 zlotys is necessary to guarantee an output of 1 zloty. The share of machinery and equipment in total expenditures is above average (42 percent). Nor will the balance of payments with the West improve, because the input of machinery and equipment from the West (45 percent of imported inputs) is much greater than the imports of machinery planned for this purpose from the CMEA (9.1 percent),[52] and because only 10 percent of the output of the projected capacities can be exported to the West. The provisions of the population will not improve to any notable degree since only 20 percent of planned production will go to mass consumer goods.

The dynamic investment activities put many industrial plants in operation, including the foundry combine at Katowice, the copper foundry Glogow II, three cement factories, four furniture factories, and the first coal mine in the new coal region around Lublin. Considerable progress was also achieved in the construction of the petrochemical combine Plock-Wloclawek and the power plant Belchatow.

The country's unprecedented investment efforts (the investment expenditures increased from 210 billion zlotys in 1970 to 610 billion zlotys in 1979 [53]) were unable to produce the planned restructuring of industrial output and the intended dynamic development of exporting enterprises. Considerable sums were invested in the raw materials industry, in which capital intensity is relatively high, but productivity, relatively low.

As in the other planned economies, construction projects limp along in Poland, and planned construction completion dates are not met (only 87 of 109 priority construction projects in the five-year period from 1971 to 1955 began operations on time), and only one-fourth of investment funds were used for modernization purposes, i.e., 50 percent less than in the industrial countries of the West.

The central authorities are able neither to resist the growing pressure from industrial management, which wants to fulfill the plans by creating new capacities, not by increasing efficiency (in the five-year period from 1976 to 1980, claims of the various industrial sectors exceeded investment projects of the central planning authorities by 800 billion zlotys), nor to enforce prompt completion of a project.

The frequent practice of beginning operations on incompleted projects in order to have a claim on bonuses has had dangerous consequences for cost expenditure and equilibrium: of 82 investment projects reviewed by the top supervisory office of the state for 1978, 60 began operations while still incomplete (barely 20 percent of the planned construction work had been carried out).

The practice of giving bonuses for spurious achievements induced the economist A. Melich to make the following statement: "If only half of the economic proceeds calculated for the obtaining of bonuses had actually been realized, Poland would certainly be a country of milk and honey."

It is noteworthy that the tremendous investment expenditure is unable to prevent bottlenecks in the utilization of production capacity. Professor Ignacy Brach has calculated that each year, machinery, equipment, and vehicles amounting to a total volume of 430 billion zlotys lie unused because replacement parts are lacking.[54]

But the main source of trouble is a false investment structure and an unprecedented waste of money. An example is the gigantic foundry at Katowice. The ex-director of the Research and Design Office Biprohut, Z. Loruth, called this project the "greatest deception": the Minister Z. Szalajda said that this foundry was to blame for the fact that at present foundry products are being imported at prices three times higher than the export prices.[55]

The cost of this foundry was estimated at 25 billion zlotys, but it has used up 120 billion zlotys, and the terms of trade for steel products have deteriorated from 1.0:1.72 to 1.0:3.23. The wide-gauge railroad between Katowice and the Soviet border is also a case in point. It cost tens of billions of zlotys, but brought about no improvement in the efficiency of transport. Other examples are the purchase of the costly Berliet license, which was of no advantage, the shutdown (because of environmental pollution) of the aluminum foundry Skawina, constructed at exorbitant cost, and, finally, the cooperation agreement with Steyr-Daimler-Puch, which never had any prospects of success.

Billions of zlotys and foreign exchange raised through credits have been wasted. Machinery valued at 50 billion zlotys, half of which has been imported from the West, has never been installed[56]; but, as the Director of Finances of the Foreign Trade Ministry, E. Harasim, has stressed, "Neither in the former nor in the present finance system had anybody noticed the severe burden of the debt, for imports on credit are free imports. Despite limits and restrictions, all have had sufficient money, not their own, but the state's."[57]

## The Energy Crisis

The unexpected, and also unplanned, boost in economic growth in the first half of the '70s created an unbridgeable gap between existing production resources and production potential, which had in the meantime been greatly expanded. The energy shortage became increasingly more acute. As the Minister of Energy, Zbigniew Bartoszewicz, stressed at the Eighth Party Congress (February 1980), much has been invested to expand the energy sector. Every year it has absorbed 10 percent of the total investments of the country, and energy capacities have increased from 14,000 megawatts in 1970 to 25,000 megawatts today. There is no shortage of energy capacity.

But poor quality is perhaps more acutely noticeable in this domain that in any other area of the economy, for 19,000 megawatts would be sufficient to meet the needs of the economy and the population. However, the bottlenecks have assumed a chronic character. Aside from the planned maintenance and repairs, capacities amounting to 2,000–2,500 megawatts are regularly shut down because of the frequent "ailments" to which power plants are vulnerable if they are not promptly renovated or prepared for the use of lower-quality coal. Much too much energy, said the minister, is wasted as a consequence of defective utilization of the machinery, and Poland's economy uses more energy than the country's level of development can justify.

The statistics also confirm that Poland uses twice as much energy, in relation to the produced national product, than Great Britain, and three times as much as France.

Often farmers waste energy simply because 1.5 kw motors are unobtainable and they must therefore use motors that are twice as powerful.

## Increasing Environmental Pollution

Environmental pollution, which has reached fearful dimensions, especially in Upper Silesia, has been cause for great concern. Zdzislaw Grudzień, former party secretary in Upper Silesia, had the following to say at the Eighth Party Congress: "Of all gases and dust emitted in Poland, 27.5 percent fall on the Katowice mining region, which makes up only 2.1 percent of the total surface area of the country." This notwithstanding, the huge Katowice foundry was built in just this region, and has caused further deterioration of the already precarious environmental situation. Each day 1,470 kilograms of dust, 800 kilograms more than can be tolerated without damage to health, fall on every square kilometer of this region. There is smog 183 days of the year, and in the areas of high population density, such as Chorzów, Swietochlowice, and Bytom, no more than 42 fog- and cloud-free days may be counted a year. The effects of this environmental pollution include severe eye diseases and many other obscure ailments of the human organism.

The rivers are hit the hardest. Ninety percent of Silesia's waterways are so polluted that their water is scarcely usable, and the

Rawa River, which runs through Katowice, has lost its liquid consistency. When it reaches its peak output in the '80s, the largest and oldest Upper Silesia coal region, which has made Poland the fourth largest coal-producing country in the world, will gradually phase out its capacities, according to a report by Z. Grudzień. The environment of this region will, however, remain polluted for a long time to come.

A shortage of water is felt not in Silesia alone, and it is not just the industrialization of the country that must bear the blame for this. The impending danger was simply not recognized in time, nor were any attempts made to undertake preventive measures. It was only after the situation had become unbearable that the Eighth Party Congress decided to regulate the Vistula, a move that was many years overdue.

This mighty river, more than 1,000 kilometers long, is, for the most part, not navigable; it has few dikes; its water is not potable. Half of Poland's arable land lies in the Vistula basin, but 20,000 towns and villwages have no water conduits, and 80 percent of all farms must obtain their water from their own wells. The reclamation of the Vistula, a program designed to extend over two decades and provide for 20–30 reservoirs, a number of locks and artificial lakes, and 35–40 inland harbors and dozens of canals, will require an outlay of 600 billion zlotys by the year 2000, i.e., about $19 billion, equivalent to the mountain of debt that has already been accumulated vis-à-vis the West. The funds will therefore not be so easy to raise.

The Wielkopolska region, with Poznan, the fourth largest city in Poland with 540,000 inhabitants, as its capital, is especially waiting for the reclamation of the Vistula. The first party secretary of this region, Jerzy Zasada, reported to the party congress as follows: "For years our region has been suffering from a water shortage, which is having an increasingly great influence on the inadequate production of foods, and for a number of years the urban and rural populations of this region have also been suffering an acute water shortage." From time to time water even had to be rationed.

## THE STRUCTURAL CRISIS IN AGRICULTURE

The property structure of Polish agriculture is a special case in the CMEA: three-fourths of the arable area is in private hands, only one-fourth being owned by the state or cooperatives. After Gomulka's comeback in 1956, the forced collectivization that had begun in the '50s was stopped. Most of the cooperatives were dissolved. But neither Gomulka nor his successors could free themselves from the thought that socialism in Poland was incompatible with private property in agriculture. The bitter experiences with forced collectivization in the first half of the '50s, the agrarian policies of neighboring countries, and the basic orientation of the state regime were unable to persuade the peasants that their existence was assured over the long term.

A paradoxical situation arose in Polish agriculture: the resistance of the peasants prevented collectivization; the party leadership accepted this situation reluctantly, but in the entire postwar period no conditions were created for a thriving growth of private plots. Another factor influencing later developments was that the agrarian reform begun in the period between the wars had been snuffed out in its very beginnings. The reform carried out just after the war was limited mainly to a nationalization of feudal lands and the lands of the Church, which were transformed into state farms (PGRs). Only a small group of peasants were able to shore up their paltry holdings. Poland's agriculture is more atomized than the agriculture in the industrial countries of Western Europe. 30.5 percent of farms have an area of 0.51–1 hectare; 30.2 percent have 2–5 hectares; and only 4.5 percent have more than 15 hectares.[58]

The share of private plots in total agrarian production in Poland was 78.1 percent in 1979.[59] However, these plots are much more poorly supplied with fertilizer and pest-control agents, building materials, and farm machinery than the state farms and cooperatives. The small plots are at best able to provide for those who cultivate them; 16.5 percent of the farms sell no farm products at all, and 29 percent sell no more than 15,000 zlotys' worth yearly.

In terms of farm machinery, Poland's capacity, which has an arable area of 19.3 million hectares, is less than that of the GDR, which has only 6.3 million hectares.[60] Poland is 20 years behind France and 15 years behind the GDR and Czechoslovakia in the mechanization of farm work.

Poland's peasants have reacted with great sensitivity to the toughening of the political climate. However, they have shown themselves to be extremely cooperative and enterprising at the least hint of liberalization. This was the case after the Polish October in 1956 and after Gomulka's fall in the first half of the '70s. Grain harvests increased from a yearly average of 20.1 centners per hectare in the second half of the '60s to 25.5 centners in the period from 1971 to 1975; the livestock count also increased considerably, from 10.8 million head in 1970 to 13.3 million in 1975. The number of hogs increased even more sharply, from 13.4 million to 21.3 million.

Favorable climatic conditions have also undoubtedly played a role. But this was surely not the only reason for the above-average harvest in the first five years of the Gierek era, just as poor weather was not the only cause of the miserable agricultural performance in the next five-year period. The change in party leadership somewhat dispelled the nightmare of impending forced collectivization. More and more signs appeared that the new party leadership was prepared to abandon its policy of autarky, which limited the importation of valuable fodder and caused immeasurable damage in the livestock sector. The supply of farm machinery, fertilizer, construction materials, coal, etc., improved perceptibly.

The thaw in agriculture did not last long, however. In the second half of the '70s, like the economy as a whole, it, too, fell victim to lack of adequate direction and to ossification and the bureaucratization of the regime. Once again the state farms were given preference, and a perceptible transfer of arable land from private property to state property occurred; this accelerated from an annual average of 34,000 hectares in the '60s to 120,000 hectares between 1970 and 1977. This transfer gave rise to a considerable restructuring of property relations: the share of the nationalized sector in arable surface area increased from 24.9 percent in 1970 to 31.8 percent in 1979, while that of the private sector decreased from 75.1 percent to 68.2 percent.[61] The restructuring in property relations had an extremely negative effect on the crop structure, since private farms cultivated much more grain and potatoes than the state farms. The peasants used 47 percent of the arable land transferred to state property for grain cultivation, but the state farms used only 31 percent of this.

The private farms were also discriminated against with regard to fodder supply: for one head of cattle, they were allotted, in 1977, no more than 389 kg, while the state farms received 1,079 kg, and the cooperatives, as much as 1,830 kg.[62] The state farms, however, used relatively more grain fodder for cattle-raising than did the peasants (the difference was 42 percent), and the total costs per unit were 40 percent higher than on private farms.[63] The undersupply of farm machinery and tools also had an extremely negative effect. The problem was particularly serious with regard to small machinery, for which there was an especially high demand. During the '70s, capacities were not enlarged, and not one supply plan was fulfilled; in the first quarter of 1981, the manufacture of farm machinery even decreased by 17 percent compared with the preceding year.

The low price for farm machinery was one of the factors blamed for the low production potential. The Ministry for Machinery Construction presented a list of 70 farm machines and tools whose prices no longer corresponded to the increase in costs. In many cases the sale price is lower than the prime cost of production, and in some cases even lower than the cost of materials. An example is a harrow, whose production cost is 3,875 zlotys, which includes 2,814 zlotys for materials, but the sale price is only 2,800 zlotys.[64] Of course, there can be no question of raising the prices of goods for peasant consumption so long as the totally fictitious price system is not restructured. The prices for basic foodstuffs have remained unchanged since 1953. In the meantime, however, the prices on the free market have more than tripled, and wages have increased eightfold (nominally). State subsidies for foodstuffs amounted to 260 billion zlotys in 1980 and about 360 billion zlotys in 1981 (as late as 1971, subsidies from the state budget amounted to no more than 17 billion zlotys).[65]

With regard to the ratio of people employed in agriculture and outside agriculture, in 1980 Poland, with a ratio of 1:2.2, ranked after the GDR (1:7.7), Czechoslovakia (1:5.4), Hungary and the USSR (1:3.3), and before Romania, in second to last place within the CMEA.

Weather conditions had an extremely negative effect on grain harvests in 1979 and on the potato and beet harvests in 1980. If, however, agricultural output was 1.5 percent lower in the second half of the '70s than in the first half, and if 35 years after World War II basic foodstuffs had to be rationed, it is the fatal agricultural policy of the government that is to blame, especially its neglect of the private sector, which today — and it is to be hoped, in the future as well — is the principal source of food for the population.

The crisis in agriculture has also had an extremely negative effect on the balance of payments. In the '70s Poland became a net importer of farm products. In the period between 1971 and 1980 the negative balance was $4,681 million.[66]

The crisis in agriculture is only one, though the most important, component in the economic crisis in Poland, and can be brought under control only by a fundamental reform in the social system.

## POLAND'S INSOLVENT ECONOMY

Poland's insolvency is not an isolated case. There are many countries in the world that have assumed more credit than they can pay back. These, however, are all developing countries. Poland, on the other hand, is one of the industrially developed nations of Europe. The country is rich in minerals and has ample resources in coal, copper, sulphur, silver, etc. Poland has suffered fewer losses from the worldwide price explosion than the other industrial countries of the West and the East, since the prices for coal and other raw materials that the country exports have also risen.

The question that must be asked is, How could it happen that a European country that has planned its economic development, attempts to shield itself from the elementary forces of the world market, has made unmistakable progress in industrialization of its economy, and certainly does not rank among the poorest countries in the world has been able to get into such a catastrophic economic situation? Even more important is the question of why Poland's insolvency caught most people, especially its creditors, by surprise, why the Polish people were surprised when they suddenly learned that negotiations had begun on restructuring the country's debt, and, moreover, under circumstances in which influential persons were even pleading for a total default of repayment. After all, Poland's insolvency was not something that occurred overnight.

The question can be answered only if we examine the peculiarities of a planned economy, for Poland is only a case in point. The per capita debt is, to be sure, greater than in the Soviet Union or Czechoslovakia, but not much greater than, for example, that in Hungary. The foreign trade system and credit practices of Poland differ little from the practices in the other Eastern countries. The core of the problem lies in the fact that the planned economies have initiated active foreign trade with the West without possessing functional mechanisms for developed multilateral trade. The foreign trade mechanisms of the Eastern countries, namely, the monopoly in foreign trade and the instruments of that monopoly, were established at a time when autarky was the growth model. The mechanisms of foreign trade are still, today, the mechanisms of an autarkic growth model in which imports are seen as stopgap measures for a meager supply by the state and exports function as a means of finacing imports that have become indispensable. They are not suited for multilateral trade with the industrial countries of the West. In the CMEA, foreign trade is cleared bilaterally, and even the founding of two international CMEA banks has been able to alter nothing in this state of affairs.

No planned economy has an economically based exchange rate, a suitable price system, and a convertible currency; with the exception of Romania and Hungary, none is a member of the Bretton Woods institutions. It is a paradox that the planned economies of Easttern Europe, which clear most of their foreign trade with their Eastern partners and sell most of their export quotas within the CMEA, are indebted mainly to the West. It must also seem a paradox that the planned economies, which regard themselves as a community of interests and coordinate their economic and foreign trade plans with one another, recognize no collective responsibility. The umbrella theory, in which the Western bankers had placed so much hope, has not functioned in the emergency. The balance of payments, the foreign exchange holdings, and the credits assumed and credits granted are everywhere regarded as state secrets of primary importance.

Not only were bankers not fully informed about economic situations, the balance of payments, and the total debt but there was simply a lack of indispensable information about the mechanisms by which the planned economies functioned. There was too much belief in the planned aspect and in the growth of the planned economies. To be sure, things were more chaotic in Poland than elsewhere; but after the orgy of growth in the first half of the '70s, the growth rates of the second half, though much lower, were regarded as satisfactory (compared with the recession in the West).

The growth of Polish trade with the West and the terms under which the unprecedented mountain of debt was accumulated show clearly how inconsistent a planned economy can be. At the beginning of the '70s the debt was no more than $764 million, and in 1971 the balance of payments with the West was positive. In the first half of the decade intensive investments were undertaken with the aid of Western credits — naturally, in the hope that the newly built capacities would permit prompt repayment of the debt. Neither creditors nor borrowers believed that they were assuming a risk when they allowed the volume of credit to rise rapidly in the following years. But it grew precipitously: by 50 percent in 1972, 92 percent in 1973, 86 percent in 1974, and 79 percent in 1975. By the end of 1975, however, the total debt was still no more than $7.4 billion — and this at a time when an unprecedented investment boom had begun and 53 percent of the new credits were used for this purpose.[67] Even then, when the debt still amounted to less than one-third of its present volume, it seemed much too high, not to the creditor countries, but to the Polish government.

In December 1975 the then Prime Minister P. Jaroszewicz declared to the Polish parliament: "We want to and must reduce the country's debt in the next five years. To achieve this goal, we must increase exports much more rapidly than imports. We assume that in the next five years imports will rise by 25 percent, but exports will increase by 75 percent." Jaroszewicz based this fine-sounding growth perspective on the favorable prospects that would be opened up by the completion of the Katowice foundry. This plant was to save no less than a billion dollars in foreign currency.[68]

The state of the debt at that time was not so alarming, although planning practice was. When investment projects were allowed to build up beyond any reasonable measure, in view of the easy access to the international money markets, it was undoubtedly not taken into consideration that the newly built production capacities would totally alter the supply structure of the economy, which would become much more import-intensive than in the first half of the '70s. The Katowice foundry saved the country no foreign exchange, but only intensified its dependence on imports.

The share of investment credits in the total volume decreased from 53 percent in the first half of the decade to 27 percent, but the share of credits for the import of raw materials, other materials, and semifinished products almost doubled in the second half of the decade and increased to 60 percent[69] of the amount of credit taken.

In not one single year has it been possible to achieve an active balance of payments. The debt became larger, as did the debt service as well. The interest grew steadily. The interest rate, 12 percent on average, was in no rational relationship to the profitability rate achievable in a planned economy. But even this none of the planners seriously considered in their calculations. The cumulative trade deficit between 1973 and 1980 was $15.2 billion, but the debt at the end of 1980 was already $23.5 billion; the difference was almost exactly equal to the interest burden. The ratio of the payment rates to the annual exports grew from year to year. In 1976 this ratio (26.3 percent) was only just barely still within the internationally acceptable standard; in 1977 it had reached 45.6 percent, and increased to 60.8 percent, 75 percent, and 83.2 percent, respectively, in the next 3 years.[70]

The concentration of the repayment debts is cause for concern. Three-fourths of the total debt is due in 1981 to 1983. This, no less than the overall economic policy, is a consequence of lack of adequate direction and of chaos in the economy. The planners fell victim to their own propaganda of success and secretiveness. Indeed, in 1978 it must have been clear that there were no prospects of covering the excessive mountain of debts in any normal way, i.e., with a foreign trade surplus. Instead of then promptly beginning negotiations to postpone repayment, new credits were feverishly assumed to pay back those that had fallen due.

# 6

# Coexistence and Cooperation Are Better than Confrontation

The social system that calls itself "socialist" is young. In the course of its historically brief lifetime, deep contradictions have emerged that seem to be insoluble within the system. It has not been able to fulfill its historical mission of creating a more just and humane civilization that could serve as an example to other nations of the world. The vision of a just communist society, which was viewed as scientifically based, has proved to be a utopia. The Russian Revolution produced what it was able to produce only under the conditions of Russian civilization and in the Russian cultural environment. There was a return to Russian civilization as it emerged historically. It was not just the French Revolution in 1789 that had its Thermidor...

There appear to be two basic causes for the Russian Thermidor: the establishment of a one-party regime, and turning of the means of production into state property. These were the prerequisites for an omnipotent state and its ruling bureaucracy. These two fundamental pillars of the system persist to this day.

The way to Thermidor was paved, above all, by abandonment of the proclaimed socialization of the means of production. Shortly after the revolution, the means of production were taken from the workers and their associations, transformed into state property, and placed under the administration of state officials. This abandonment of the objectives of the October Revolution had a decisive influence on the shaping of the social structure. A classless society was no longer a plausibility. The ruling classes of the *ancien régime*, the capitalists and large landowners, were replaced by a much more powerful stratum of state bureaucrats, who extended their control into all areas of social life. The broad class of yesteryear, the workers, has remained a class of wage laborers. The shaping of the class structure was brought to a close when the land was taken from the peasantry, collectivized, or transformed into state property.

Property relations and the class structure determine the mode of production. It is not capitalistic: no private owners control the social product, but neither do the immediate producers. Separation of the producers from the means of production persists, as do the hierarchical relations of authority. There are no longer any free trade unions that could have a say in the distribution of the social product. The state has suppressed the market as well as tried-and-proven market mechanisms. The economy is centrally administered, not steered by means of economic laws. High growth rates do not give rise to a corresponding improvement in well-being. The development model is of decisive importance, and in it heavy industry and the armaments industry have priority.

The other attributes of "real socialism" were hammered out in the aftermath of World War II, when the nationalist ideology of the great Russian Empire was recast in the Marxist heritage. Suvorov and Kutusov, the field marshals of Catherine II and Alexander I, were made heroes of the "Soviet Nation"; and Russian traditions, culture, and the Russian language were brought increasingly to bear in the cultural landscape of the Soviet Republics. The victory was used to expand the Soviet sphere of influence over Eastern and Southeastern Europe. The Soviet Union, which acted in accordance with the absolutist principle of "Cuius regio eius religio," legitimated its expansionist policies not only through its need for security but also through the aspirations of the proletarian world revolution, as defined in the constitution of 1924. It stated: "All workers of the world shall be united in a soviet world republic."

None of the promises of the October Revolution has been fulfilled, but the ideology of Marxism-Leninism remains inviolable for the Soviet Union. It is needed, for "A dictatorship cannot act in its own name. It must hide behind an ideology" (Karl Popper). For internal consumption it serves as a promise of a better future in communism; it also serves, however, for external consumption, as the ideology of a great power that seeks to justify its territorial conquests as "fraternal aid" and "international commitments."

## REAL CONTRADICTIONS IN REAL SOCIALISM

While Stalin lived, the contradictions in his regime of power were suppressed with terror. Khrushchev's revelations at the

Twentieth Party Congress (February 1956) on the horrifying methods of rule of his predecessor exceeded all that even the most zealous anticommunists had said.

Shortly after Stalin's death, on 17 June 1953, the first revolt against the Stalinist system occurred in East Germany. The mass unrest in Poland and the popular uprising in Hungary followed three years later. Then came the "Prague Spring," after a somewhat greater passage of time, in 1968, and, finally, the more recent mass unrest in Poland in 1970, 1976, and 1980 and their issue in a chronic economic and political crisis. The methods of rule against which the revolts were addressed cannot be explained by the individual personality traits of the great dictator and his pettier epigones. They are the inevitable consequence of a one-party dictatorship.

The "Nomenklatura" — the party apparatus, the economic management, and the cultural officials — have no common interests with the workers and the peasants. The French essayist Maurice Duverger has justly commented: "The workers in the Soviet empire are scarcely less exploited by the *apparatchik* entrepreneurs than the workers in the West by capitalist entrepreneurs, and the privileges of the 'Nomenklatura' derive from surplus value just as do the profits of the owners of the means of production."[1]

Furthermore, the gap between the conditions of existence of the rural and urban populations remains just as wide as that between the divergent interests of the ruling bureaucracy and the workers, who can hardly be said to have anything in common. The peasant has not advanced to the status of the city dweller, but rather has been degraded to the status of a wage laborer. Moreover, he is far more meagerly equipped with mechanical tools than his colleague in the industrialized West. Also, he produces less. With the exception of Hungary, the Eastern countries, which before the agrarian revolution were known as the bread basket of the rest of the world, have become net importers of grain.

The economies of these countries show unmistakable signs of crisis. The times of above-average growth rates are past. But the boom was interrupted at a time when there was still a considerable discrepancy between the relatively high level of development and the relatively low living standard of the population, and gaps in supply had still not been closed. The political leadership is, moreover, unwilling to alter the growth structure at the expense of the arms industry and to the benefit of the manufacture of consumer goods. If, nonetheless, some of the planned economies still show greater growth rates than the market economies, it is understood better in the East than in the West that there is no comparison between growth in production to fulfill a plan and growth to satisfy a competitive and open market.

It is becoming ever more clear that a centrally administered economy can be prosperous only if it has an abundance of cheap material resources and labor power at its disposal. The planned economies achieved their greatest successes at a time when it was important to produce as much coal, ore, steel, cement, etc., as possible and to build factories beyond number. However, they are not able to develop a brain-power-intensive, modern, commodity production in which individual initiative is of decisive significance.

Given the poor quality of their goods and their meager communication mechanisms, the planned economies cannot be regarded as partners of equal status in the highly developed Western market. Their steering mechanisms, which acquired their final form in the period of autarkic development, are unable to function as a codetermining factor in the world market. The preference for bilateral clearing, which invariably reduces exchange to the capacities of the weaker partner, persists in intra-CMEA trade and has shaped trade with the West.

In modern technology and modern know-how, the planned economies are net importers; in credit relations with the West, they are borrowers, not lenders. Poland and Romania are insolvent; Bulgaria, the GDR, and Hungary have already borrowed more than their economies can bear.

The Eastern countries are entering the '80s with a tremendous mountain of debt, which for some of them is the equivalent of the value of two to four years of exports:

| | Bulgaria | CSSR | GDR | Poland | Romania | Hungary | USSR |
|---|---|---|---|---|---|---|---|
| a) Debt (net) at end of 1980 (billions of dollars) | 4.0 | 3.8 | 10.3 | 23.0 | 7.9 | 8.4 | 7.5 |
| b) Exports to the West, 1980 (millions of dollars) | 1,322 | 3,244 | 3,944 | 5,921 | 3,640 | 2,898 | 24,541 |
| Ratio a:b (in percent) | 302 | 117 | 261 | 388 | 217 | 290 | 30 |

*G. Fink, _An Assessment of European CMEA Countries' Hard Currency Debt._ Vienna, September 1981.

The Eastern bloc has been unable to reduce its backwardness relative to the Western industrial countries. In 1970 the average per capita income (in 1980 prices, expressed in terms of buying power) of the Eastern bloc countries was $2,540, whereas that of the industrial countries was $7,000; in 1980 these figures were $3,720 and $8,960, respectively. The estimates for 1990 of $4,950 and $11,700, respectively, are unfavorable for the Eastern countries.[2]

The contradiction between arms production, which makes up no less than 12–14 percent of the national product, and production for the needs of the population, still unsatisfied, is becoming more acute. This clearly shows how heavy a burden the arms race has been for the Eastern countries. Assuming spending to be equivalent on both sides, the arms burden of the East is twice as heavy to bear as that of the West since the former's national product is only half as large.

A development model oriented toward heavy industry and the arms industry stands in sharp contradiction to the demands of the population for consumption that matches the achieved level of development. The inclination to consume increases as the official ideology becomes an empty shell. Just as development into an industrial society has become an inevitability, development into a consumer society should also be inevitable. The Eastern countries have already overtaken the West in alcohol consumption. Less and less are the people allowing themselves to be lured by the promise of a happy future under communism.

The moral decadence of the ruling elite and the corruption of those in power are the most conspicuous features of "pure socialism." A dreadful example was provided by the ruling elite in Poland swept away by the workers' uprising of 1980: among the 3,422 state officials whom the country's Supreme Chamber of Control found guilty of misappropriation in the construction of private homes were three Central Committee secretaries, 23 first secretaries of regional committees (the total number was 49), 7 vice-prime ministers, 18 ministers, 56 vice-ministers, 21 _voivods_ (regional heads), and 30 vice-_voivods_.[3] This inclination of people who belong to the elite to enrich themselves, draw high salaries, and enjoy numerous privileges is not characteristic of the ruling stratum in Poland alone; it is visible in any Eastern country. In early October 1981, the Soviet Central Committee journal _Sotsialisticheskaya Industriya_ reported on the dismissal of E. Chalikov, vice-minister for the crude oil and gas industry, who had no time for his ministerial duties because he had so many side occupations and had neglected his principal activity to such a degree that considerable losses had accrued. Chalikov had half a course at the Moscow School for the Petrochemical and Gas Industry, appropriated the paid expertise orders of a research institute, and neglected to pay all the party contributions. The ministry lost a total of 36 million rubles. Such examples may also be found in the other Eastern countries.

Neither the autarkic policy of former days nor the intensification of economic relations with the West, begun in the '70s, has created the conditions necessary for technical progress. It has been found that progress cannot be imported. Not only has a considerable debt been accumulated but dependence on developments worldwide has become greater. Today the Eastern countries, poor in energy resources, are suffering just as much from the price explosion as the other countries of the world. The circumstance that the smaller countries of the East procure their fuels mainly from the Soviet Union has not been able to mitigate their economic problems to any significant extent since the Eastern bloc receives not only modern economic know-how, but also modern communications mechanisms from the West. Inasmuch as the autonomously structured national price systems of the individual countries diverge appreciably from one another, there has been no possibility of creating a special price scale for intrabloc trade. The price system is borrowed from the West, although not without limitations. Thus, according to a decision of the Ninth Congress of the CMEA in May 1958, prices were to be freed from "cyclical, seasonal, speculative, and other distortions" of the capitalist market. An average price, determined on the basis of price fluctuations in the preceding five-year period, was to be used in the following five-year period. However, after the price explosion of October 1973 shook the world, a sliding price scale for every year was introduced, in early 1975, under pressure from the Soviet Union. Hence, inflation sets in with some delay. The exorbitantly high price of oil, which exceeded the extraction costs by 20–100-fold, was dumped by the Soviet Union on the shoulders of its partners in the CMEA and the Warsaw Pact. The Soviet Union did not become much richer thereby, but the smaller countries of the East became much poorer. They have so far been unable to make up the foreign trade deficit to which this gave rise.

The reactions to developments worldwide also clearly demonstrate the structural weaknesses of the planned economies. Their adaptability is much less than that of the market economies. Professor Wolfram Engels has aptly remarked: "...In the '70s the Western industrial countries embarked upon a whole series of false paths based on false theories, yet our open societies show a high degree of problem-solving ability and adaptability. In the East it has not yet been learned that the socialist theories have failed."[4]

Inflation immediately affected the internal price systems of the market economies and resulted in structural adaptations in both production and consumption. The effect of the price explosion has been devastating: adaptation is still flawed. Nonetheless, the mechanisms continue to function. OPEC, the strongest monopoly of the '70s, has been forced to capitulate.

In the planned economies, on the other hand, there is no direct communication mechanism that can channel the price developments worldwide to the domestic market. The new situation must be digested by the state bureaucracy. There is a general unwillingness to call the parameters of the five-year plan into question. Adaptative measures, though indispensable, are put off as long as possible. Enterprises continue to show profits, although they have long produced losses. The state budget fills the gap and distorts economic accounting. Fictitious parameters make a cost-benefit analysis more difficult. Enterprises and private consumers remain shielded from economic pressure. Though there have been appeals to econmize and conserve, their effectiveness cannot be compared with the situation of an entrepreneur who must struggle for existence in a competitive market.

The price shock hit the smaller states of Eastern and Southeastern Europe harder than it did the market economies, not only because the meager communication mechanisms were unable to send out signals of an impending malaise, but because the specific expenditure of energy and raw materials was much higher than elsewhere. The economic upswing of some of the planned economies, accompanied by a growing use of imported raw materials and fuels, was still going on even after the advisability of a curb on imports and economic growth had become obvious. For example, Poland did not dampen its growth euphoria until 1976. A growing scarcity of resources and an unsupportable mountain of debt and debt service have been the consequences. The economic and political system that had brought progress to the Eastern economies in the first phase of industrialization, by dint of enormous expenditure of labor power and material resources, is showing structural cracks in its present phase of development.

## A CHAOTIC STRUCTURAL TRANSFORMATION

Conflicts are accumulating at a perceptible rate, but the conflict-resolving potential is insufficient. The interplay between challenge and response (Arnold Toynbee) functions poorly when there is no competition in politics and economics.

At this stage, when the structural flaws of the social system have become obvious, it is becoming increasingly clear how wrong it was to impose an economic and political system molded under the specific conditions of post-czarist Russia upon the countries of Eastern Europe, with their completely different structures. In the Soviet Union this system was at least a product of internal conditions. It is more a typically Russian phenomenon than a product of the ideas of a utopian socialism. The population has had enough time to get used to the system in the Soviet Union, and the ruling stratum has superbly mastered the techniques of the exercise of power. The patriotic component is increasing steadily in importance. Although all elements of the Marxist intellectual tradition have failed in confrontation with hard realities, pride in the achievements of the Soviet fatherland has remained a motivating factor. And if the living standard is still much below that in the industrial nations of the West that have developed economically in a similar direction, it has nonetheless increased considerably in the last 20 years.

The situation was, and is, different in the smaller nations of Eastern Europe. The social system, imposed from without, is still perceived as an alien element. These countries have indeed made considerable progress in industrialization, but the cost in terms of quality of life is too great. In these countries, too, there has been a certain pride in the achievement of the "socialist fatherland." But national sensibilities have been much too deeply wounded by "proletarian internationalism," i.e., Soviet hegemony.

General reforms have been introduced, but they have been much more timid in the Soviet Union than in the small nations. The Soviet authorities have never permitted the central powers to lose control of the economy. Although planning techniques and the organization of administration have improved considerably over the course of time, the economic system itself has not changed. A few countries with planned economies have dared to undertake radical changes in the economic steering system, under pressure of mass movements, but they have never been able to "maintain order in the midst of change, and change in the midst of order" (Josef Schumpeter). This applies both to the revolutionary movement in Poland and Hungary in 1956, to Czechoslovakia in 1968, and, especially, to events in Poland in 1980 and 1981. The geopolitical factor has played a decisive role in the suppression of these revolutionary movements, for the Soviet leadership is convinced that the maintenance of "universally valid rules of order" is an indispensable precondition for Eastern integration.

The features the reform movements in Poland and Hungary in 1956, the "Prague Spring" in 1968, and the Polish mass movement of 1980 and 1981 have had in common are striking. In all of them, a reexamination of the great ideals of democratic socialism is discernible, and nowhere is a tendency toward restoration of the _ancien régime_ to be noted. The objectives are that a truly social ownership of the means of production should replace state property, that bodies of self-management should replace the hierarchic bureaucracy in economics and politics, and that an institutionalized group pluralism should reflect the pluralistic division of society.

The fundamental ideas of the democratic reform movements have been expressed most clearly by the great reformer and thinker Oskar Lange. When he was able to express his opinion freely after the stormy "Polish October" of 1956, he wrote: "Poland's economic system, a socialistic economic model, must be adapted to the historical and geographic conditions of the country. It cannot be invented on the green desk of authority, but must be the creation of the great movement for socialist democracy that has swept the country." Lange believed that decentralized economic powers, the right of the workers to codetermination, self-administered cooperatives, and self-administrative bodies for the peasants must be the basic pillars of a reformed social system. "The renewal will be the result of the passionate ideological engagement of the young intelligentsia and their search for a means to replace a command economy with effective economic mechanisms."[5]

The radical democratic reformers of Poland and Hungary in 1956, and those of Czechoslovakia in 1968, wanted to transform the central steering of enterprises, which left only a slight margin of freedom for exercising initiative, into a system of true enterprises that made their own decisions concerning production, sales, and development. They wanted to "loosen" the economic system so as to create conditions under which workers could fully develop their creative forces and be rewarded according to performance. They wanted to put an end to the notion of happiness fashioned from above. It was at that time that the slogan 'Democratization by the people, not for the people" was coined. A self-administered enterprise was seen as a microcommunity led by a feeling of collegial cooperation and working in its own interests for the good of society.

None of the reformers attempted to present a complete model of a new system. The final contours of a just yet efficient social system would crystallize in the process of renewal. There was no uniform opinion on the relationship of workers to the means of production. However, it must be expressly emphasized that not one serious reformer, neither then nor now, wanted to reprivatize the means of production, although they did want to free them from the administrative control of the state bureaucracy. Oskar Lange was prepared to accept the Yugoslavian model of decentralized decision-making powers, but he was not prepared to transfer ownership of the means of production directly into the hands of the enterprise collective. In his opinion, every plant was supposed to be a trustee of that part of the total national assets placed in its hands and bear full responsibility for its productive use.

In the years of the great upheaval, Hungary's reformers had no time to allow their notion of a future economic and political order to mature. Imre Nagy, the unfortunate prime minister in the difficult days of the Budapest uprising, had wanted to democratize the political system and then to decentralize economic control. The idea of the self-administered enterprise was unanimously accepted; such an enterprise was to make its own decisions concerning production within the framework of a state plan that was to have more of an indicative than an imperative function. The workers' councils that had sprung up spontaneously at the time were also to have a voice in all matters concerning enterprise operations. Hungary's reformers in 1956 intended to modify the growth model of the economy. Forced industrialization had, in their opinion, deformed the economic structure and resulted in profound disproportionalities. They planned to invest more in agriculture and to curb collectivization.[6]

The Prague Spring sketched the contours of a reformed economic system more distinctly, and perhaps even more radically, than the reformers in Poland and Hungary in 1956. Autonomy of enterprises, their independence of the state and party organs, was the basic principle of the reform model. Only a very narrowly circumscribed group of enterprises of importance to the state was to be controlled directly by the ministries. Most of the economic units were classified as "public property," and were to function independently of state organs. In these enterprises workers' councils were to control production and sales, and only a minority of enterprise managements were to be appointed by a body consisting of representatives of ministries, banks, and other organizations. Most were to be freely elected. Small-scale industry was to be converted into cooperative or private property.

The Czech enterprise law, which never became operative, for well-known reasons, explicitly stressed that enterprises themselves were to decide on the associations to which they wished to belong and that industrial corporations were to have no administrative powers. Enterprises were to be granted the right to decide, voluntarily, whether to join an industrial association, or to leave it.[7]

This retrospective glance over the reform movements in the three most important states of Eastern Europe has been necessary to show that just as the ruling elite in the small Eastern countries has sometimes copied Soviet institutions to the letter, so, too, does the authentic workers' movement necessarily hark back to the Russian experiences with workers' councils in the year of revolution 1917. It is not democratic socialism, which has never been realized, but "real socialism" that is rejected.

## PROSPECTS

The successes and failures of the reform movements indicate the direction of future development. The radical movements of 1956 in Hungary and of 1968 in Czechoslovakia were brought to an end by outside forces. Thus have the geopolitical limits of radical transformations under real socialism become visible. The Polish reform plans of 1956 were later killed by the party leadership itself, which, like the party leadership in Czechoslovakia in 1968, had placed itself at the head of the mass movement in the first phase. This makes the limits of a reform initiated by the party visible. Discontent, however, remains, and the reform movement does not subside.

Since the revolutionary events of the mid-'50s and the end of the '60s, the developments in Poland, Czechoslovakia, and Hungary have diverged. Twelve years after the Budapest uprising, the Hungarian party leadership, under Janos Kadar, initiated an economic reform under party control. Economic powers were broadly decentralized, administrative mechanisms were, to a considerable extent, replaced by traditional market mechanisms such as money, credit, prices, exchange rates, etc.; and political conditions were perceptibly liberalized. Today, Hungary seems to be the best governed and perhaps the most stable country in Eastern Europe, enjoying a relatively broad accord between rulers and ruled. But it remains a party dictatorship, if a very enlightened one. There is no striving for a utopian life-style; instead, the model of a capitalist consumer society is the goal of aspirations.

After the Prague Spring, Czechoslovakia reverted to the traditional system. Peace and order reign, but a pervasive apathy and conformist passivity that are not conducive to the economic and cultural development of the country prevail.

In Poland, the stability that set in after the reform movement was throttled was of but short duration. The power structures and methods of rule restored during the '60s led to a revival of the reform movement toward the end of the decade. In December 1970, Gomulka, first a protagonist and then a liquidator of the ambitious reform plans of former days, was overthrown by a workers' uprising on the Baltic coast. Other party leaderships, however, were able to bring the revolutionary movement under control and to steer development into traditional channels, with the usual negative consequences for society and the economy. The growth euphoria, fueled by Western credits, gradually developed into a supply crisis that ultimately led to a political crisis, a crisis of the system.

The events of 1980 and 1981 differed essentially from those of the '50s. For the first time in the history of Eastern Europe, independent trade unions were formed that fought, by traditional means, for the traditional rights of the working class. The legend of a "classless workers' state" was dispelled before the eyes of the world public in the second largest country of the Eastern bloc. On the one hand, the aristocracy of the party establishment, the powerful "Nomenklatura," defended its privileged position; on the other, the working class fought for its class interest. All the underpinnings of the established social system began to shake. It should be noted that these are the same underpinnings that sustain the social system in the other East European countries.

The common characteristics of the mass movements of 1956 and 1980–1981 are unmistakable: "Poland's October (1956) was not a palace revolution," said one of the most active participants, E. Lasota. "It was a social movement of the underprivileged, led by ideologically motivated members of the party, often against the will of the party as an institution."[8] The same features were discernible in Poland's workers' movement in 1980–1981. However, it was more consistent: not only in the formulation of its reform proposals but in the organization of resistance. It had become richer by the experience of October 1956 and, especially, December 1970, and poorer by the illusions it had then entertained. It was not going to leave the fate of the reform in the hands of the party leadership, as it had done before. The issue was to establish and institutionalize a pluralistic social order; it aspired to what the critical Marxist philosopher Adam Schaff proposed: "...a weakening of the bureaucracy by structurally preventing its concentration in a single center of power....the formation of a number of autonomous, relatively independent apparatuses competing with one another..."[9]

With his coup d'état of December 1981, General Jaruzelski put an end, temporarily, to these aspirations. He had given in to the pressures of the Soviet leadership, which still thought that a uniform social system in all the countries of Eastern Europe was the best guarantee of the cohesion of the Eastern bloc. The Soviet Union still preferred tutelage to good neighborly relations, relationships such as exist, for example, between it and Finland, which have brilliantly withstood the test throughout the postwar period.

A protective wall of neighboring states with a similar social system around the Soviet Union will certainly not be useful in a confrontation with the West. It is becoming increasingly more expensive for the Soviet Union, both materially and morally. Good relations with its neighbors without any claim to hegemony, and abandonment of the confrontational policy with the West would be more supportive of the Soviet Union's exaggerated need for security than the continuing arms race with the economically stronger West. Expansion for reasons of security is just as dangerous for peace as expansion for reasons of "fraternal aid." The world public sees no difference between these two forms of expansion: and this is true of the strongest Communist Parties in Western Europe as well. Discarding the fortress mentality would have a decisive influence on the growth model of the Soviet Union. The best human forces and the scarce material resources would then not be used for military purposes, but for raising the still low living standard of the population. Means for creating a material basis for a higher stage of society could then be released. A just social order would serve to propagate the socialist ideal better than the construction of military bases in foreign countries, which condemn millions of people to a refugee's existence without making the others happier.

Lucio Lombardo Radice was right when he said: "Really existing socialism — we are thinking primarily of the Soviet model — is a fundamentally different system than that sketched in Marxist socialist theory, for one basic reason: in the Soviet model the state as a separate body not only does not die but is growing, with a tendency to control everything, and is becoming all-powerful."[10]

Unfortunately, the creators of this all-powerful state forgot the warning of the great Russian exile philosopher Nikolai Berdyaev: "The state does not exist to transform life on earth into a paradise, but to prevent it from becoming a hell."[11]

There is no reason to expect that a state economy in the industrialized West would look essentially different from that of Eastern Europe. On this point Adam Schaff says: "Goodwill and conviction alone are not sufficient, as is believed in broad circles of Communist Parties in the West, as a guarantee that 'we' would do it better because 'they' are incapable of achieving the desired results because of their low level; we, however, are something different." Schaff rejects this view emphatically, for "the belief in the 'level' is illusory; moreover, with the present structure of our system, the negative phenomena giving us concern cannot be avoided."[12]

Marxism no longer generates "a true political, cultural, philosophical, and pedagogical Sturm und Drang movement" as in the past epoch (Radice). When Marx wrote his monumental work, the world population was only a third its present size. At that time the steam engine was still almost the only source of power in industry. Civilization was still far removed from its present production and destruction potential, natural resources were still essentially intact, the environment was clean, and the world was not divided into two hostile systems.

An efficient world order, conceived as a framework of communication for thriving economic and cultural cooperation, can be established without the two world systems' altering their fundamental principles. The Western social system, with its tremendous civilizing contribution and its social achievements, does not deserve to be destroyed, and "real socialism" does not deserve to be spread. Only coexistence and cooperation between the two world systems can save civilization from the catastrophe that threatens it as a consequence of the continued arms race; the ministries of defense of all countries pay more than 200 million people, directly or indirectly.

I should like to close with the warning that more than 200 scientists and scholars of all disciplines addressed to the United Nations from Menton: "We must henceforth see the world, which until now has seemed inexhaustible, in its limitedness. We live in a closed system; we are totally dependent on one another and on the earth; and this is true both for our lives and for the lives of coming generations. All that separates us is much less important than that which unites us, and this is the primary danger facing us."[13]

# Notes

## CHAPTER 1

1. Központi Statisztikai Hivatal, Magyar statisztikai zsebkonÿv, 1966. Budapest. P. 39.
2. Comment by the former Prime Minister of Hungary, András Hegedüs, in Wiener Tagebuch, January 1980.
3. See Gospodarka planowa (Warsaw), 12/1979.
4. Csikós-Nagy at the Assembly of the German Southeastern Europe Society (Frankfurter Allgemeine Zeitung, 6 March 1981).
5. See "Hungary, the Quiet Revolution." The Economist, 20 November 1980, p. 54.
6. See János Fekete, "The Crisis of the International Monetary System and the Hungarian Economy." The New Hungarian Quarterly, 21 (79) 33, 34.
7. Ibid., p. 34.
8. Studies have shown that in the branches that make up 70–75 percent of industrial output, competitive price formation can be introduced (see Béla Csikós-Nagy, "Die ungarische Wirtschaftspolitik." Europäische Rundschau (Vienna), 3/1980, p. 5.
9. Béla Csikós-Nagy, op. cit., p. 56.
10. J. Fekete, op. cit., p. 39.
11. See Béla Csikós-Nagy, [ "Reform of the Price System"]. Zycie Gospodarcze (Warsaw), 6 August 1980, p. 9.
12. Ibid.
13. Ibid.
14. Béla Csikós-Nagy, "Die ungarische Wirtschaftspolitik." Europäische Rundschau, 3/80, p. 51.
15. See Viktor Meier, "Budapest besteht auf seinem eigenen Weg" (A talk with the National Bank President Timar, Frankfurter Allgemeine Zeitung, 9 October 1980).

16. J. Fekete, op. cit., p. 40.
17. See G. Aczél on politics in Hungary, Europäische Rundschau (Vienna), 80/4, p. 4.
18. See Maria Dabrowska, [ "The Hungarian Economic Mechanism in Confrontation with the Economic Problems of the '70s"] . Gospodarka planowa (Warsaw), 2/1979, p. 682.
19. See National Foreign Assessment Center, Estimating Soviet and East European Hard-Currency Debt. Washington, D.C., June 1980.
20. Frankfurter Allgemeine Zeitung, 10 September 1980.
21. The Economist, 20 November 1980: ("Hungary — The Quiet Revolution"), p. 71.
22. M. Ushievich, [ "Hungary's Economic System"] . Planovoe khoziaistvo (Moscow), October 1980.
23. RFE-Research, 19 December 1980.
24. See the monthly Partelet (Budapest), 3/1981.

## CHAPTER 2

### The German Democratic Republic

1. Deutsches Institut für Wirtschaftsforschung, Handbuch der DDR-Wirtschaft. Hamburg, Rowohlt, November 1977. P. 19.
2. Ibid., p. 22.
3. Statistisches Jahrbuch 1980 für die BRD, p. 710.
4. See O. K. Flechtheim, "Kommunismus in Deutschland 1918–1975." In the anthology Die Sowjetunion, Solschenizyn und die westliche Linke. Hamburg, Rowohlt, 1975. Pp. 98, 99.
5. See Boris Ponomarev, [The History of Soviet Foreign Policy from 1945 to 1970] . Moscow, 1974. Pp. 364, 365.
6. O. K. Flechtheim, op. cit., p. 97.
7. Statistisches Jahrbuch der Deutschen Demokratischen Republik 1979, p. 1.
8. Deutsches Institut für Wirtschaftsforschung, Handbuch der DDR-Wirtschaft. P. 26.
9. W. Ulbricht, "Die weitere Gestaltung des gesellschaftlichen Systems des Sozialismus." Speech at the 9th Congress of the Central Committee of the SED. Berlin, 1968. P. 39.
10. See Der Spiegel, 3/1978, p. 26.
11. Quoted in Frankfurter Allgemeine Zeitung, 31 October 1979

("Unausrottbare Tonnenideologie").

12. All the countries of Western Europe, plus Australia, Japan, Canada, New Zealand, and the USA.
13. Statistisches Jahrbuch der Deutschen Demokratiochen Republik 1979, (data for 1978), p. 232.
14. U.S. Department of Commerce, U.S.-GDR Trends. Washington, D.C., April 1981.
15. Wochenbericht des Deutschen Institutes für Wirtschaftsforschung, 6/81.
16. See National Foreign Assessment Center, Handbook of Economic Statistics 1980. Washington, D.C., October 1980. Table 2.
17. Ibid.
18. National Foreign Assessment Center, Estimating Soviet and East European Hard-Currency Debt. Table A-10.
19. See Wochenbericht des Deutschen Institutes für Wirtschaftsforschung, 12/81.
20. See Frankfurter Allgemeine Zeitung, 27 August 1981.
21. See Radio Free Europe Background Report 220, 3 August 1981.
22. Günter Mittag, "Kombinate im Kampf um die Durchfuhrung der okonomischen Strategie des 10. Parteitages." Einheit, June 1981, p. 531.
23. Informative data may be found in the article by Angela Scherzinger, "Aspekte der neuen Planungsordnung in der DDR," in the quarterly report of the Deutschen Institut für Wirtschaftsforschung, January 1981.
24. "Die DDR — despotischer Staatsozialismus." Der Spiegel, 42/1978.

Czechoslovakia

1. See Pawel Bozyk, Współpraca Gospodarcza Krajów RWPG (Economic Cooperation in the CMEA). Warsaw, 1977. P. 31.
2. Ibid., p. 30.
3. Ibid., p. 35.
4. See Zbigniew Brzezinski, The Soviet Bloc, Unity and Conflict. Cambridge, Mass.: Harvard University Press, 1960. P. 86.
5. Klement Gottwald, Spisy 12 (Collected Works, Vol. 12). Prague, 1955. Pp. 253–54.
6. Quoted in Karel Kaplan, Znárodnine al socialismus (Nationalization and Socialism). Prague, 1968. P. 211.

7. Ibid.
8. See N. Ivanov, [ "The Foreign Trade of the People's Democracies"]. Vneshniaia torgovlia (Moscow), October 1952.
9. See Zbigniew Brzezinski, op. cit., p. 91.
10. O. Kyn, "Die tschechoslowakische Wirtschaftsreform und ihr Ende." In the anthology Die Wirtschaftsordnungen Osteuropas im Wandel. Freiburg, 1972. P. 141.
11. Rudé Právo, 8 December 1952.
12. J. Pjekalkiewicz (Ed.), Public Opinion Polling in Czechoslovakia 1968/69. New York, 1972.
13. Hansjakob Stehle, Nachbarn im Osten. Frankfurt, 1971. P. 82.
14. Peter Hruby, Fools and Heroes. The Changing Role of Communist Intellectuals in Czechoslovakia. Oxford, 1980.
15. Information on the economic reforms in Czechoslovakia can be gotten from R. A. Remington, Winter in Prague. Cambridge, Mass., 1969; and O. Kyn, op. cit.
16. See O. Kyn, op. cit., p. 176.
17. See Zdenek Mlynář, Nachtfrost, Erfahrungen auf dem Weg vom realen zum menschlichen Sozialismus. Cologne-Frankfurt, Europäische Verlagsanstalt, 1978.
18. Plánované hospodárstvi, 5/1970, p. 7.
19. See Pawel Bozyk, op. cit., p. 31; and National Foreign Assessment Center, Handbook of Economic Statistics. Washington, D.C., October 1980. P. 11.
20. Ibid., pp. 10, 11.
21. United Nations, Economic Survey of Europe in 1980. Geneva, 1981. P. 156.
22. Ibid., p. 158.
23. Wirtschafts- und Sozialstatistisches Taschenbuch 1981. Prague. P. 241.
24. United Nations, op. cit., p. 119.
25. See Die Presse, 1 July 1980.
26. Wochenbericht des Deutschen Institutes für Wirtschaftsforschung, 25/81.
27. United Nations, op. cit., p. 130.
28. Rudé Právo, 29 July 1981.
29. See Pravda (Bratislava), 11 July 1981, p. 3.
30. Pravda (Bratislava), 22 July 1981, p. 13.
31. Tribuna, 29 April 1981, p. 13.
32. Statisticka Ročenka (CSSR) 1978 (Prague) p. 403; Statisticka Ročenka (CSSR) 1980, p. 418; Rudé Právo, 23 January 1981.

33. Wochenbericht des Deutschen Institutes für Wirtschaftsforschung, 25/1981.
34. National Foreign Assessment Center, Estimating Soviet and East European Hard-Currency Debt.
35. See Wochenbericht des Deutschen Institutes für Wirtschaftsforschung, 25/1981.
36. U.S. Department of Commerce, East–West Trade Policy, U.S.–Czechoslovak Trade Trends. Washington, D.C., April 1981.
37. Ibid.
38. See Handelsblatt, 19 September 1979 (talk with A. Barcak, Foreign Trade Minister of Czechoslovakia).
39. Wochenbericht des Deutschen Institutes für Wirtschaftsforschung, 25/1981.
40. Prague telegraph agency, 12 September 1980.

CHAPTER 3

1. P. Bożyk, Współpraca Gospodarcza Krajów RWPG (Cooperation of the CMEA countries). Warsaw, 1977. P. 31.
2. Ibid.
3. See J. Giezgala, "Die Industrialisierung Osteuropas und die internationale Arbeitsteilung." In the anthology Aussenhandel und Wirtschaftswachstum der RGW-Länder. Warsaw, 1969. P. 28.
4. See National Foreign Assessment Center, Handbook of Economic Statistics 1980. Table 2.
5. See P. Bożyk, op. cit., p. 31.
6. Ibid., p. 36.
7. See National Foreign Assessment Center, Handbook of Economic Statistics 1980. Tables 1 and 2.
8. Felipe Garcia Casals, The Syncretic Society. New York, 1980. P. 5.
9. See Y. Gluckstein, Stalin's Satellites in Europe. London, 1952. P. 15.
10. See Z. Brzezinski, The Soviet Bloc, Unity and Conflict. Cambridge, Mass.: Harvard University Press, 1960. P. 99.
11. Enzykopädie des Wissenschaftlichen Staatsverlages. Warsaw, 1973. P. 374.
12. Z. Brzezinski, op. cit., p. 86.
13. Ibid., p. 16.
14. See N. Ivanov, [ "Foreign Trade of the People's Democracies

of Europe"]. Vneshniaia torgovlia (Moscow), October 1952.
15. See Vilko Chervenkov, "The Activities of the Bulgarian Workers Party." For a Lasting Peace, for a People's Democracy (Prague), March 1947, p. 2.
16. See V. Dedijer, Tito. New York, 1952. P. 318.
17. Rabotničesko Delo, 4 December 1965.
18. Daržaven vestnik, 14 March 1969.
19. Quoted in Heinrich Vogel, "Rollen und Entwicklungen der Wirtschaftsreform in Bulgarien seit 1965." In the anthology Die Wirtschaftsordnungen Osteuropas im Wandel. Freiburg, 1972. Vol. I, p. 228.
20. Ibid.
21. See Rabotničesko Delo, 5 May 1981.
22. See Ikonomičeski Život No. 2, 2 June 1976.
23. Albania, Bulgaria, Czechoslovakia, GDR, Cuba, Mongolia, North Korea, Poland, Romania, USSR, Hungary, Vietnam, and the People's Republic of China.
24. National Foreign Assessment Center, Estimating Soviet and East European Hard-Currency Debt.
25. Ibid.
26. U.S. Department of Commerce, U.S.–Bulgarian Trade Trends. Washington, D.C., April 1981.
27. See Ikonomičeska Misl, 1/1980.

## CHAPTER 4

1. See Zbigniew K. Brzezinski, The Soviet Bloc, Unity and Conflict. Cambridge, Mass., 1971. P. 443.
2. Ibid., p. 125.
3. Those who, like the author of these lines, were able to observe the stubborn resistance of Romania to any form of collective property in the CMEA at close hand know quite well that these sad experiences with the Sovroms were the main cause.
4. Ana Pauker, Vice Prime Minister, Foreign Minister, and Central Committee Secretary, and Georgescu were never brought to trial; V. Luca was sentenced to death and then received clemency. He died in prison. The sentence was annulled in September 1968.
5. Quoted in Hansjakob Stehle, Nachbarn im Osten. Frankfurt, 1971. P. 171.

6. Ibid., p. 167.
7. See Hansjakob Stehle, op. cit., p. 187.
8. Ibid.
9. See Michael C. Kaser, "Rumänien: Die Vervollkommung von Planung und Leitung der Volkswirtschaft." In the anthology Die Wirtschaftsordnungen Osteuropas im Wandel. Freiburg, 1972. Vol. 2, p. 261.
10. Ibid., p. 255.
11. Scinteia, 14 December 1969.
12. See National Westminster Bank, Romania: An Economic Report. London, June 1981.
13. Anuarul Statistic al Republicii Socialiste Romania 1980. Bucharest.
14. Ibid.
15. See National Westminster Bank, op. cit.
16. Anthony Robinson, "Ceausescu promises jam tomorrow — or by 1990." Financial Times, 27 November 1979.
17. See Neue Zürcher Zeitung, 24 June 1981 ("Stärkere Handelsverflechtung Rumäniens mit Moskau").
18. Gross investments in percent of national income.
19. See Wochenbericht des Deutschen Institutes für Wirtschaftsforschung, 25/81.
20. Ibid.
21. United Nations, Economic Survey of Europe in 1980. Geneva, 1981. P. 106.
22. Anuarul Statistic al Republicii Socialiste Romania 1980, pp. 113, 363.
23. United Nations, op. cit., p. 99.
24. Ibid., p. 92.
25. See Wachenbericht des Deutschen Institutes für Wirtschaftsforschung, 25/81.
26. United Nations, op. cit., p. 108.
27. Ibid., p. 112.
28. Frankfurter Allgemeine Zeitung, 5 November 1981.
29. National Foreign Assessment Center, Estimating Soviet and East European Hard-Currency Debt. P. 11.

CHAPTER 5

1. This manifesto was published by Verlag Philipp Reclam jun.,

Leipzig, 1976. P. 25.

2. Quoted in Erik-Michael Bader, "Nachdenken über den Nachbarn Sowjetunion." Frankfurter Allgemeine Zeitung, 18 March 1981.
3. In a discussion of party intellectuals in Krakow, February 1981.
4. Stefan Kisielewski, "Striptease in Polen." Der Spiegel, 18/1981, p. 52.
5. Quoted by Stefan Kisjelewski, ibid.
6. See P. Bozyk and B. Wojciechowski, Handel Zagraniczny Polski (Poland's Foreign Trade) 1945–1969. Warsaw, 1970. Pp. 17, 18.
7. See B. Kieseweter, Der Ostblock. Berlin, 1960. P. 36.
8. See P. Marer, "Soviet Economic Policy in Eastern Europe." In Compendium of Papers, submitted to the Joint Economic Committee of the Congress of the United States. Washington, D.C., 16 August 1974. P. 140.
9. Rocznik Handlu Zagranicznego (Foreign Trade Yearbook). Warsaw, 1974.
10. See Zycie Gospodarcze (Warsaw), 2 July 1978.
11. N. Fadiejew, RGW (CMEA), Moscow, 1974. P. 22.
12. Mały Rocznik Statystyczny 1939 (Warsaw), p. 96.
13. Ibid.; Mały Rocznik Statystyczny 1936 (Warsaw), p. 54.
14. See S. Lewy, [Estimates of Nonagricultural Unemployment from 1929 through 1936]. Warsaw, 1939. Appendix I.
15. See Zycie Gospodarcze (Warsaw), 2 July 1978.
16. Mały Rocznik Statystyczny 1939 (Warsaw), p. 198.
17. Ibid.
18. Ibid., p. 31.
19. Ibid., p. 103.
20. Ibid., p. 10.
21. Ibid., pp. 27, 29.
22. Ibid., p. 70.
23. Ibid., p. 68.
24. See Zycie Gospodarcze (Warsaw), 2 July 1978.
25. Ibid.
26. In 1935 the illegal Communist Party of Poland (exluding the Western Ukraine and Western White Russia) had 7,421 members. See J. Kowalski, Kommunistische Partei Polens 1935 bis 1938. Warsaw, 1975. P. 68.
27. Of course, Poland's economy was based on the achievements of science, but as the Krakow sociologist Piotr Sztompka wrote:

"State power was based on science like a drunk on a light pole: it sought no light, only support and something to hold on to." Quoted in Wiener Tagebuch, III/1981, p. 11.
28. See M. Kucharski, Pieniadz, Dochod, Proporcje Wzrostu (Money, Income, and Growth Proportions). Warsaw, 1964. Pp. 254, 255.
29. Ibid., p. 255.
30. See Biuletyn Institutu Gospodarki Narodowej (Report of the Institute of National Economy). Warsaw, July 1948. P. 20.
31. See Rocznik Statystyczny 1961 (Warsaw), p. 172.
32. See K. Laski, "Warunki rownowagi ogolnej miedzy produkcja a spozyciem w gospodarce socjalistycznej" (Conditions of equilibrium between production and consumption in a socialist economy). In the anthology [Problems of Poland's Socialist Economy]. Warsaw, 1954. P. 216.
33. [Materials on the 8th Conference of the Central Committee of the PUWP]. Warsaw, 1956. P. 17.
34. M. Kucharski, op. cit., p. 266.
35. Quoted in Der Spiegel 19/1981, p. 200.
36. See M. Kucharski, op. cit., p. 327.
37. Rocznik Statystyczny 1971 (Warsaw), p. 133.
38. Ibid., p. 202.
39. See M. Rakowski, Przesilenie grudniowe (The turning point in December). Warsaw, 1981.
40. Quoted in M. Rakowski, ["Conclusions for the '80s"]. Polityka (Warsaw), 14/1981.
41. See Trybuna Ludu, 8 May 1981.
42. See Polityka (Warsaw), 2 June 1979.
43. Rocznik Statystyczny 1977 (Warsaw), p. 288.
44. Ibid., p. 289.
45. See Polityka (Warsaw), 16 May 1981.
46. See A. Plocica, "Manewr inwestycyjny w gospodarce (Investment maneuvering in the economy). Inwestycje i budownictwo, Warsaw, 12/1977.
47. J. Pajestka, Determinanty postepu (Factors determining progress). Warsaw, 1975, p. 263.
48. A. Karpiński, "Rola polityki uprzemyslowienia kraju" (Industrialization policy of the country). In [Thirty Years of Poland's Economy]. Warsaw, 1974. P. 122.
49. See Rocznik Statystyczny 1980 (Warsaw), p. 68.
50. See Trybuna Ludu, 2 May 1981.

51. See J. Macieja, [ "Engagement in Investment and Frozen Investment Projects"]. Gospodarka Planowa, 1/1981.
52. Ibid.
53. Rocznik Statystyczny 1971, p. 149; Rocznik Statystyczny 1980, p. 120.
54. Ignacy Brach, [ "Innovations"]. Przeglad Techniczny (Warsaw), 15/1981.
55. See Polityka (Warsaw), 9 May 1981, p. 4.
56. See Handel Zagraniczny (Warsaw), 11/1980, p. 7.
57. See Polityka (Warsaw), 21 February 1981.
58. Rocznik Statystyczny 1980, p. 245.
59. Ibid., p. 213.
60. See R. Fafara, [ "Demogogy and Agriculture"]. Zycie Gospodarcze, 5 March 1981.
61. See Rocznik Statystyczny 1980 (Warsaw), p. 213.
62. See Z. Kozlowski, Socialism and Family Farming. London, Social Science Research Council.
63. Ibid.
64. See J. Boldak, ["What Is Paying Off"]. Zycie Gospodarcze, 24 May 1981.
65. See E. Fiala, [ "Cheap Food, but at What Price?"]. Trybuna Ludu, 10 April 1981.
66. See A. Lubowski, ["Where Were the Billions Lost?"]. Zycie Gospodarcze, 3 May 1981.
67. Ibid.
68. Quoted in M. Gajewski, [ "Plans and Indebtedness"]. Trybuna Ludu, 6 May 1981.
69. See A. Lubowski, op. cit.
70. Ibid.

CHAPTER 6

1. Maurice Duverger, "Le socialisme du troisième type." Le Monde, 21 July 1981.
2. Handelsblatt, 20 October 1981.
3. Polityka (Warsaw), 14 July 1981.
4. Professor Dr. Wolfram Engels, in a speech given before the European Forum in Alpbach in 1981; see Die Presse, 19–20 September 1981.
5. See Trybuna Ludu, 31 December 1956.

6. For details on Hungary's reform plans in 1956, see Imre Nagy, On Communism: In Defense of the New Course. New York, 1957.
7. A detailed description of the reform movement of 1956 is to be found in R. A. Remington, Winter in Prague, Cambridge, Mass., 1969.
8. E. Lasota was head editor of the most radical press organ of the reform movement in the mid-'50s, Po Prostu. See Polityka (Warsaw), 24 October 1981.
9. Adam Schaff, [ "Socialism and Bureaucracy"] . Polityka (Warsaw), 4 October 1981.
10. Lucio Lombardo Radice, op. cit., p. 126.
11. Quoted in Le Monde, 26 September 1978.
12. Ibid.
13. Quoted in Aurelio Peccei, Die Zukunft in unserer Hand. Vienna, 1981. P. 25.

# Index

# About the Author

Born in Poland, Adam Zwass for many years held managerial positions in the central banking systems of Poland and the USSR. From 1963 to 1968 he was Counsellor in the CMEA Secretariat in Moscow, where he was responsible for financial settlements and the work of the International Bank for Economic Cooperation.

Since his emigration to Vienna in 1969, Dr. Zwass has been affiliated with the German Institute of Economic Research (West Berlin), the Austrian Institute of Economic Research (Vienna), and the Viennese Institute for Comparative Economic Studies. He is currently active as a bank advisor.

Dr. Zwass is the author of numerous articles on monetary questions, banking, and problems of integration, which have been published in Europe and in the United States. His books include *Wielkość i struktura obiegu pieniężnego* (Warsaw, 1962), *Pieniądz dwóch rynków* (Warsaw, 1968), *Zur Problematik der Währungsbeziehungen zwischen Ost und West* (Vienna, 1974; published in English as *Monetary Cooperation Between East and West* by M. E. Sharpe, Inc., New York, 1975), and *Money, Banking and Credit in the Soviet Union and Eastern Europe* (White Plains, New York and London, 1979). In 1982 he published *Planwirtschaft im Wandel der Zeit*. *The Economies of Eastern Europe in a Time of Change* is an abridgment of that book.

For Product Safety Concerns and Information please contact our EU
representative GPSR@taylorandfrancis.com
Taylor & Francis Verlag GmbH, Kaufingerstraße 24, 80331 München, Germany

www.ingramcontent.com/pod-product-compliance
Ingram Content Group UK Ltd.
Pitfield, Milton Keynes, MK11 3LW, UK
UKHW021122180425
457613UK00005B/183